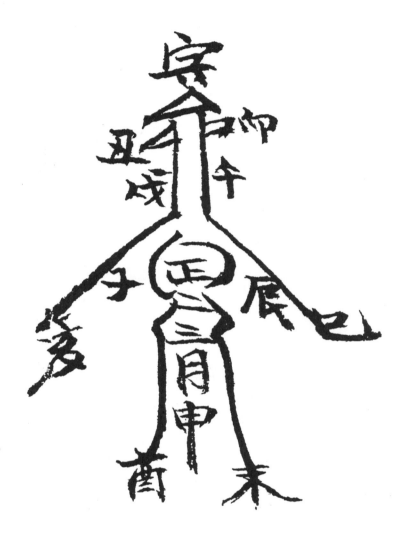

KOREA, Scenic beauty & religious landmarks

KOREA, Scenic beauty & religious landmarks

Mark De Fraeye
Frits Vos

KOREA

Scenic beauty
& religious landmarks

PANDORA

(endpapers) *Figure-pictograms with notations of times-of-day, used for predictions. From an old shamanistic manuscript.*

(cover)*A stone pagoda (6 meters high) from the mid-Koryŏ period, Mirŭng-ni (< Mirŭk-ri), Koesan county, Ch'ungch'ŏng Pukto.*

(back cover) *Doors painted with flower and leaf motifs in Sinhŭng-sa, a Sŏn temple on the east slope of Sŏr'ak-san (not far from the east coast) in Kangwŏn-do. The temple dates originally from 652, but was rebuilt for the third time in 1648.*

(pages 6–7) *Halla-san National Park on Cheju-do.*

(pages 8–9) *Door to the shrine where the memorial tablet of Admiral Yi Sunsin (Korea's great 16th-century naval hero) is preserved. It is part of the Hyŏnch'ung Shrine near Onyang. The doors are decorated with an emblem representing the two cosmic forces* ŭm *and* yang *(Chinese* yin *and* yang*); the circle symbolizes the Great Absolute,* T'aegŭk *(Chinese* T'ai-chi*).*

(pages 10–11) *Monk opening the door to one of the buildings of the Pulguk-sa, Kyŏngju, Kyŏngsang Pukto.*

(pages 12–13) *The dragon's head motif is both shamanistic and Buddhist. Part of a wall panel in Changgok-sa, Ch'ŏngyang county, Ch'ungch'ŏng Namdo.*

(pages 14–15) *Fisherman's son waiting for his father to return from the sea. Ullŭng-do.*

(page 16) *Detail of a folk painting. The crane stands for longevity and represents one thousand years of life.*

© 1996 Mark De Fraeye (photographs), Frits Vos (text) and Pandora

D/1996/5890/10
ISBN 90-5325-052-2

Publishers: Petraco – Pandora nv, Antwerp

Printed in Belgium

AGFA *Agfa*

Photographs
Film: Agfachrome 100RS (120)
Camera: Hasselblad 500 CM
Lenses: 50, 80, 150 mm, SWC 38 mm

Contents

For Bieke and Michan

Preface

This book is not a travel guide, although we hope it will encourage some of its readers to get to know the beautiful country of Korea on their own.

When we use the name Korea here, we are almost always referring to the Republic of Korea (South Korea). The few photographs that show a little of the North Korean landscape (Paektu-san) were taken from the north (from Manchuria) on a trip De Fraeye took there.

We were quite limited in the amount of text we could fit into the book. Consequently there are no separate sections on art and literature. In the section on history, however, we have paid some attention to these topics.

De Fraeye takes the responsibility for the choice of illustrations. They are arranged according to aesthetic considerations and not chronologically. Vos is responsible for the text, including the captions.

No one writes a book alone or – as in this case – with two persons. Of the friends who have assisted us in word and deed, we will only be able to mention a very few.

Mark De Fraeye would like to thank Dr. Chang Kyung-ho for his expert advice. For the sensitive and critical eye with which Dr. Cheon Ok-kyung followed the development of the project, he would like to express his thanks. To Hyun Ho Sunim he is grateful for accompanying him on his search for the roots of Korean culture. Special thanks are expressed to the D. Sadowitz family for their hospitality and constant solicitude.

Grateful acknowledgement is also made to the Korean Overseas Information Service. He is particularly indebted to Bartel Baccaert whose encouragement and belief in this book added an extra dimension to the final outcome. Finally he owes much to the unfailing support of his wife and children through all the months of work and long absences from home.

Frits Vos wishes to thank his wife Miyako and his daughter-in-law Djie Myong Soek for preparing the examples for the section 'Language and writing system.' He would like to express his gratitude to his old friends, Mrs. Byoungnim Choi, Prof. Daiwon Lee (painter and until a few years ago rector of Hong Ik University) and Prof. Young-Hwan Oh (Department of Philosophy, Yonsei University), for everything he has learned from them over the course of the years.

Together we would like to thank Mrs. Katherine Dege for her faithful and very readable English translation, Mr. Antoon De Vylder for the beautiful layout and the supervision of this book's production and Mr. André Bollen, director of Pandora, for his personal interest in our project and the pleasant collaboration.

Our most grateful thanks also go to Mr. René Peeters, member of the Board of the Agfa-Gevaert group for his enthusiastic and relentless support for this project. Without this invaluable help this publication would not have materialized.

Mark De Fraeye
Frits Vos

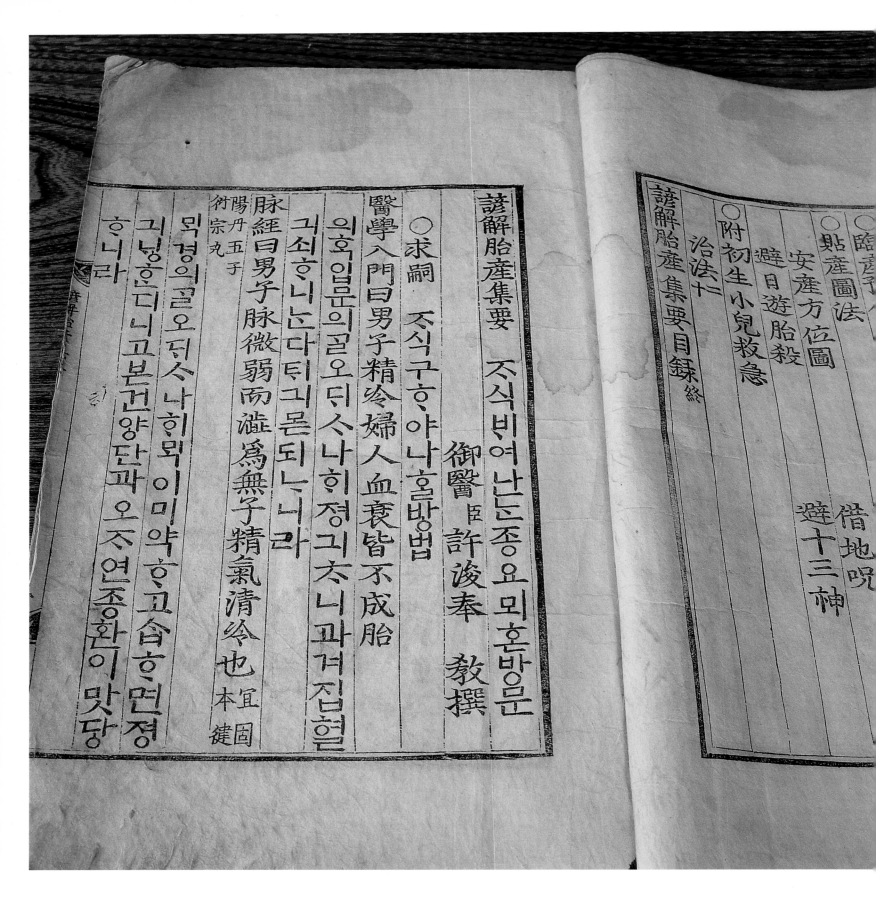

First page of Ŏnhae T'aesan chib'yo, 'The Essentials of Parturition Explained in Korean Script', by the famous medical scholar Hŏ Chun (1546-1615), published in 1608. On the right side of the photograph, part of the table of contents (in Chinese characters) is visible; on the first page itself the Chinese title in the right-hand column and the following Chinese sentences are accompanied by Korean translations in han'gŭl (old spelling)

Transcription and pronunciation of Korean words

*T*he transcription system we use in this book is the internationally recognized McCune-Reischauer Romanization system (1939). In this transcription the consonants are pronounced as in English, the vowels as in 'continental' languages (i.e., German or Italian).

Vowels

a	like *a* in *father*
i	similar to *ee* in *beet*, but not drawn out
o	similar to *o* in *tow*, but not drawn out
ŏ	similar to *u* in *hut* or *aw* in *awful*
u	similar to *oo* in *boot*, but not drawn out
ŭ	similar to *u* in *hush* or *usher*
ă	short *a*, occurs only in older texts
Yi	the usual transcription of the family name I (Chinese: Li), pronounced like *i* (cf. above)

Diphthongs and Triphthongs

ae	*(a + i)*	like *a* in *hat* or *e* in *bed*
wa	*(o + a)*	like *wa* in German *Volkswagen*; the phonetic value of *w* is, however, similar to the English 'double u'
oe	*(o + i)*	similar to *we* in *well*, or (sometimes) to *oeu* in French *coeur* but not drawn out
e	*(ŏ + i)*	Similar to *a* in *aid*, but not drawn out
wi	*(u + i)*	similar to *we*
wŏ	*(u + ŏ)*	similar to *wo* in *won*
ŭi	*(ŭ + i)*	*ŭ + i* spoken rapidly, sometimes sounds almost like *oi*, but usually like just *i*, esp. in *hŭi* (like Eng. *he*); the genitive particle *ŭi* sounds like *ai* in *air*
wae	*(o + a + i)*	similar to *we* in *wear*
we	*(u + ŏ + i)*	similar to *wai* in *wait*

The reader should further note the pronunciation of *e + u* and *ŏ + u* (which are two separate syllables, not diphthongs according to Korean phonology), e.g., *Cheu* (a personal name) is pronounced *Che-u*; *Sŏul* (= Seoul) is pronounced very much like the English word *soul*.

Consonants

b, ch, d, g, h (cf. below) are pronounced like in English; *k, m, n, p, s,* and *t* also like in English, but unaspirated, i.e., not accompanied by a puff of air.

j	like in *jam* or *jazz*
l	similar to *l* in *letter*, i.e., a 'light' *l*
r	similar to *r* in British *very*, i.e., with one flap of the tongue
w	like *w* in *well* (cf. *wa* above)
y	like *y* in *year*
ng	like *ng* in *ring*

ch', k', p' and *t'* are aspirated, i.e., accompanied by a marked exhalation of air.

Furthermore note:

k, p and *t* at the end of a word are implosive; i.e., there is no *h* sound after them, as often in English.

h before the semivowel *w* (e.g., *hwa* or *hoe*) sounds like a bilabial [F].

s before *i* is pronounced like English *sh* (e.g., *sin = shin*)

gye, hye and *kye* are pronounced *ge, he* and *ke*.

The double consonants *kk, pp, tt* and *tch* (= *ch + ch*) sound rather like *g, b, d* and *j* pressed out with the throat muscles highly tensed; *ss* is a hissing *s*.

Examples

kyŏul (winter): kyaw-ool; *Paekche* (name of a country): Pekchay; *Silla* (name of a country): Shilla; *Ch'oe* (family name): Chwe; *hye* (favor): hay; *segye* (world): saygay; *Kyerim* (= Silla or its capital): Kerim; *kukhoe* (parliament): kookFwe; *Munhŭi* (girl's name): moonhee; *Yi Hyegu* (name of a musicologist): eehaygoo; *haksaeng-ŭi ch'aek* (the student's book): hakseng-ay chek.

For the transcription of Chinese words we use the Wade-Giles system and for Japanese that of Hepburn, both with the customary modifications.

Language and writing system

Language

There are several hypotheses regarding the genealogy of the Korean language, but it is usually included in the Tungusic group of the Altaic languages (which comprise the Turk languages and the Mongolian and Tungusic language groups).

Over the course of centuries a large number of words from the – unrelated – Chinese language were absorbed into the Korean language and adapted to its phonetic system (we shall deal with the phonetic system in the section on the writing system). In a modern six-volume dictionary we find a total of 160,000 words, of which 85,000 are of Chinese origin. These words are referred to as 'Sino-Korean.' In other countries belonging to the Chinese culture area, e.g., Japan and Vietnam, there are likewise Sino-Japanese and Sino-Vietnamese words.

Because these words were borrowed at different times and from different parts of China, the Sino-Korean pronunciation differs significantly from the modern Chinese pronunciation. In the following list the modern Chinese pronunciation is given in parentheses:

hakkyo, school (hsüeh-hsiao)
Kongja, Master K'ung, Confucius, (K'ung-tze)
munbŏp, grammar (wen-fa)
sajŏn, dictionary (tz'e-tien)

In addition to these borrowings from the Chinese there are loanwords from other languages. Many of these words were adopted from the Japanese during the colonial period (1910-1945), e.g.:

alk'ol, alk'ool, alcohol (Portuguese: alcool)
ppang, bread (Portuguese: pāo)
chŭk'ŭ, linen, cloth (Dutch: doek)
mesŭ, dissecting knife (Dutch: mes)
sŭp'oit'ŭ, syringe (Dutch: spuit)

There are also many Sino-Korean (originally Sino-Japanese) translations from the Dutch, e.g.,

maengjang, appendix (Dutch: blinde darm)
piik, wing of the nose (Dutch: neusvleugel)
pyŏngwŏn, hospital (Dutch: ziekenhuis)†

Most modern borrowed words come from English:

naip'ŭ, knife
p'ainaep'ŭl, pineapple
pŏsŭ, bus
t'ellebijŏn, television

One also finds examples of self-made English, e.g., Nyuk'ŏmbaek, 'New come back,' as the name of a bar.

Typologically Korean is an agglutinating language, although the verbs have certain inflectional features. In the ancient language vowel harmony definitely existed, and it has not yet completely disappeared.

In its grammatical structure Korean is very close to Japanese; its phonetic structure is fundamentally different, however. There are very few possibilities for identifying related words. Undeniably related are:

Korean	Japanese
chŏt	chichi, breast, breast milk
kom	kuma, bear
mŭl (modern: mul)	mizu (*midu), water
pae, ship	*pe in *pesaki (modern hesaki), (mar.) stem
syŏm (modern sŏm)	shima, island

An example of the similarity between the sentence structure of the two languages:

(Kor.) Kanan-han nongbu-nŭn so-ga ŏpsŭmnida
(Jap.) Binbō-na hyakushō-wa ushi-ga arimasen

Meaning: The poor farmer has no ox (literally: speaking of the poor farmer, there is no ox).

Kanan-han nongbu and Binbō-na hyakushō both mean 'poor-being farmer' (the farmer, who is poor); nŭn and wa mark the so-called absolute case: speaking of … (the poor farmer is being contrasted with other farmers); so, ushi = ox; ga marks the subject; ŏpsŭmnida, arimasen = there is not. In both languages the verb is at the end of the sentence. The syntactic functions of the parts of the sentence are marked by postpositions.

The Korean language knows neither gender nor articles, and in general it does not make any distinction between singular and plural:

saram, the person, a person, [the] persons. If the plural is to be emphasized, the particle -tŭl (-dŭl) is attached to the noun: saram-dŭl, [the] persons.

A distinction is often made between 'neutral' or humble and polite or respectful nouns:

anae, one's own wife	puin, madam, the wife of the person addressed
chip, house (in general)	taek, house of a higher ranking person, your house
mal, (my) words, speech	malssŭm, your words

† Between 1639 and 1854 only the Dutch were allowed to carry on trade with Japan. In the eighteenth century and the first half of the nineteenth century the Japanese eagerly studied European science via the Dutch language and adopted or translated many words.

ttal, (my) daughter   *ttanim*, the daughter of a superior, your daughter

Verbs do not distinguish between persons, unless polite or humble forms or polite verbs are being used. Depending on whether the person one is speaking to is higher or lower in rank or the same rank as oneself, a friend, or a child, different verb endings are used, e.g.:

iri wa, come here! (to a child or housemaid)

manhi chapsusipsio, I hope you enjoy the meal (literally: please, eat a lot!)

In modern speech five or six different language levels can be distinguished.

Almost any verb can be made into a polite form by inserting the infix *-si-* between the stem and the ending, e.g., *kada*, to go – *kasida*, to go (said of a higher ranking person); *alda*, to know – *asida* (the person spoken to).

There are also a number of special polite verbs, e.g.:

chada, to sleep *chumusida*, to sleep (said of a higher ranking person)

chukta, to die *toragasida* (actually: to return)

itta, to be there *kyesida*, to be there (said of a higher ranking person)

mŏkta, to eat *chapsusida*, to eat (said of a higher ranking person)

There are only very few true adjectives. Most English adjectives correspond to so-called verbal adjectives, which have also been referred to as verbs of attribution, qualitativa or neutral verbs, e.g.:

k'ŭda, to be big; *nappŭda*, to be bad

The participles of these verbal adjectives correspond to English adjectives used attributively:

i chib-i k'ŭda, this house is big (the *p* of *chip* is voiced when it precedes a vowel).

k'ŭn chip, the big house (actually: the house that is big)

nappŭn saram, the bad person (the person who is bad)

True adjectives are *oe* (only, single), *sae* (new) and *yet* (former, earlier):

oe adŭl, the only son

sae chip, the new house

yet mal > yenmal, (1) archaic word, (2) old proverb

There is no declination in the Korean language, as we have seen, but certain particles are attached to the noun as postpositions to mark the nominative or possessive case, etc.:

haksaeng-ŭi ch'aek, the student's book (*ŭi*, pronounced *e*, is the possessive marker).

abŏji-ga ai-rŭl sarang-hamnida, the father loves the child (*-ga* is the subject marker, *-rŭl* is the object marker).

Let us turn to sentence structure. The verb always stands at the end of the sentence. Attributives precede that to which they refer (hence the attributive possessive and the adjective always precede the subject, the adverb the verb); adverbs of time and place can stand at the beginning of a sentence; subordinate clauses precede the main clause.

Yojŭm-e-nŭn Han'guk-saram-ŭn chunghakkyo-ttae-but'ŏ tarŭn nara-ŭi mar-ŭl pujirŏnhi paeunda, 'Nowadays Koreans diligently learn foreign languages starting in middle school.' Word by word the sentence says: nowadays-in *(yojŭm-e)*-speaking of *(-nŭn)* Koreans *(Han'guk-saram)*-speaking of *(-ŭn)* middle school *(chunghakkyo)*-time *(ttae)*-starting from *(but'ŏ)* other countries *(tarŭn nara)*-of *(ŭi)* languages *(mal)*-object marker *(ŭl)* diligently *(pujirŏnhi)* study. An absolute case is used twice here (*-nŭn* after a vowel, *-ŭn* after a consonant): nowadays is compared with former times, the Koreans are contrasted with persons from other countries. The object marker is *-rŭl* after a vowel, *-ŭl* following a consonant: *mal-ŭl > mar-ŭl*.

Writing System

In ancient times the Koreans had no other writing system besides Chinese characters, and books and other documents were written in classical Chinese, i.e., in a language that was not related to their own.

Over the course of time a way of writing was developed in which some Chinese characters were used logographically (to represent nouns, verb stems and so forth) and some phonetically (to indicate the pronunciation of Korean particles, verb endings, etc.). In this manner it was possible for Koreans to write in their own language. It was a very awkward method, however, and therefore was not used to any great extent.

The role of classical Chinese in Korea and Japan is comparable to that of Latin in Europe – with the reservation that in both countries Chinese was used only as a literary language and not in conversation.

Some examples of Chinese characters are:

人	言	信	日	昔	鳥	鵲
a	b	c	d	e	f	g

a man, mankind: side view of a person walking. Sino-Korean pronunciation: *in*, Korean pronunciation: *saram*.

b words, speech: a mouth (the square at the bottom), out of which words (the four lines on top) flow. Sino-Korean *ŏn*, Korean *mal*

c a compound of a (abbreviated form) and b: 'a man and his word' = faith, trust. Sino-Korean *sin* (trust, confidence), Korean *mitta* (believe in, trust).

d a stylized depiction of the sun. Sino-Korean *il*, Korean *hae* (sun), *nal* (day).

e pieces of meat skewered on sticks (the upper part of the character) and hung in the sun (bottom) to dry, which are therefore *old*. Sino-Korean *sŏk*, Korean *yet*. Meaning: formerly, ancient times.

f drawing of a bird. Sino-Korean *cho*, Korean *sae*.

g compound of e and f: a bird, whose name sounds approximately like *sŏk* (e is the so-called phonetic element of this character). Sino-Korean *chak*, Korean *kkach'i*. Meaning: magpie. The explanation of the pronunciation does not quite apply here, but one must of course consider the ancient Chinese pronunciation of e and g (in Sino-Japanese both characters are usually read as *jaku*).

For c compare 'Religions and Philosophy' (p 167, r.), for f 'Mythology' (p 116, r.).

Around the middle of the fifteenth century the Korean alphabet *(han'gŭl)* was invented (cf. History, p 89). In July 1940 a hitherto unknown but undoubtedly authentic text of the 'correct sounds to instruct the people' *(Hunmin chŏng'ŭm)* was discovered in a private house in Andong. This book (registered as National Treasure No. 432) contains an 'Explanation of the Creation of the Letters,' which we have consulted for our further remarks.

In the following table the consonants are combined into five groups according to their articulation (the letters that are no longer in use today are in parentheses).

ㄱㅋ ㄴㄷㅌㄹ ㅁㅂㅍ ㅅㅈㅊ(ㅿ)

k k' n t t' l/r m p p' s ch ch'

ㅇㅎ(ㆁㆆ)

ng h

The letter *k* shows the shape of the back of the tongue closing the throat. For the aspirated *k (k')* a stroke is added.

The letter *n* shows the shape of the tongue touching the back side of the front teeth or the front palate. The shape of *t* is of course particularly meaningful. For the aspirated *t (t')* again a stroke is added.

The letter *l/r* represents the movement of the tip of the tongue when articulating these consonants.

The letter *m* shows the shape of the mouth (it is also the Chinese character for 'mouth'). The shapes of *p* and *p'* are derived from this symbol.

The letter *s* represents the shape of the front teeth. For the aspirated *ch (ch')* again a stroke is added.

The circle in the last group of consonants represents the shape of the throat. Preceding a vowel at the beginning of a word or syllable the first consonant of this group is always written, but not spoken (cf. the *spiritus lenis* in Greek); at the end of a syllable it is pronounced *ng* (like in 'long').

One can rightfully describe the consonants in *han'gŭl* as 'visible speech.'

The five groups of consonants correspond to our velar, dental, labial, fricative, palatal and glottal consonants. Not illogically, the Koreans include the liquid sound *r/l* among the dental consonants).

The voiced consonants *g, d, b* and *j* are positional variants of *k, t, p* and *ch*. Between two vowels and after *m, n* and *ng* the unvoiced consonants are almost always voiced: *Chung + kuk > Chung'guk* (China), *pa + ta > pada* (sea), *ka + ta > kada* (to go), *Kyŏng + chu > Kyŏngju* (name of a city).

Following an *l*, *t* and *ch* usually remain unvoiced, e.g., *hwaltong* (activity), *ilchŏn* (recently). With other consonants one can never be sure, cf. e.g., *mulkogi* (fish, literally water meat) and *pulgogi* (barbecue, literally fire meat).

The interior of a pharmacy in Seoul. The superscriptions are all in han'gŭl; *half-a-century ago they would have been in Chinese characters*

within a word. Between two vowels it is pronounced *r*, at the end of a syllable *l*, e.g., *nara* (country), *mul* (water).

A typical feature of Korean is the many euphonic changes to which the consonants are subject: $k + m >$ *ngm*, e.g., *Han'guk-mal* (the Korean language) > *Han'gungmal*; $p + m >$ *mm*, e.g. *sip-man* (10 x 10,000 = 100,000) > *simman*; $m + r >$ *mn*, e.g., *tam-ron* (discussion) > *tamnon*.

The double consonants (cf. 'Transcription and Pronunciation of Korean Words') are:

ㄲ	ㄸ	ㅃ	ㅆ	ㅉ
kk	tt	pp	ss	tch

The vowels are:

ㅏ	ㅑ	ㅓ	ㅕ	ㅗ	ㅛ	ㅜ	ㅠ	ㅡ	ㅣ	(ㆍ)
a	ya	ŏ	yŏ	o	yo	u	yu	ŭ	i	(ă)

Originally they were written differently:

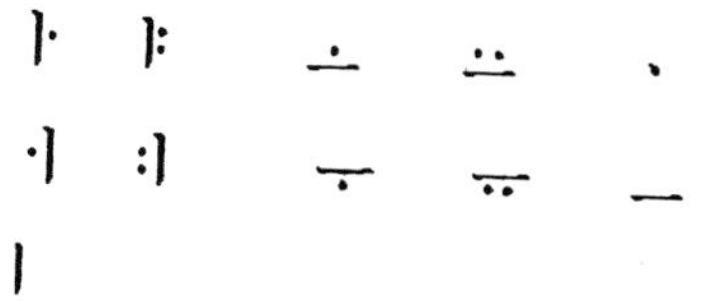

Here we have intentionally listed them in a different order. In the first line the dots in the first four letters *(a, ya, o, yo)* lie outside of or above the line and therefore come from heaven (the last character in this line, *ă*, originally only a dot, itself represents heaven, which is round). Consequently they are male *(yang)*. In the second line the dots in the first four letters *ŏ, yŏ, u, yu)* lie inside or under the line and therefore come from earth (the last character, *ŭ*, itself represents earth). Consequently they are female *(ŭm)*.

The male vowels in the first line correspond to our back vowels, the female ones in the second line to our front vowels. This difference is important in connection with vowel harmony (cf. below). The letter *i* in the third line represents man, who stands between heaven and earth. It is neutral and can be combined with vowels from either group.

The diphthongs and triphthongs are:

ㅐ	ㅒ	ㅔ	ㅖ	ㅘ	ㅙ	ㅚ	ㅝ	ㅞ	ㅟ	ㅢ
ae	yae	e	ye	wa	wae	oe	wŏ	we	wi	ŭi

In *wa* $(o + a)$, *wae* $(o + a + i)$, *wŏ* $(u + ŏ)$ and *we* $(u + ŏ + i)$ we find examples of vowel harmony.

In writing and printing the letters are arranged in syllable complexes that can almost look like Chinese characters to the uninitiated:

나라	바다	사랑	서울	미국	한국
nara	pada	sarang	sŏul	Miguk	Han'guk

Nara, 'country'; *pada*, 'sea'; *sarang*, 'love'; *sŏul*, 'capital, Seoul'; *Miguk*, 'America'; *Han'guk*, 'Korea.'
A person can learn the Korean alphabet on a rainy afternoon. Learning Korean orthography requires intensive study, however.

Names

All Koreans have Chinese names, though they are pronounced in a Sino-Korean manner. Like in China and Japan, the surname, or family name *(sŏng)*, is written first and the given name *(myŏng,* our first name) last.

The first president of the Republic of Korea, Yi Sŭngman, called himself Syngman Rhee, however, and thus rendered his name in the Western style. Two of the country's later presidents, Pak Chŏnghŭi and No T'aeu, adhered to the East Asian style and wrote their names Park Chung Hee and Roh Tae-woo.

The family name 'Yi' (pronounced like *ee* in *beet*) corresponds to the Chinese 'Li.' It is variously transcribed by persons whose name it happens to be as Yi, I, Li, Lee, Ree, Rhee, Ri, Rie, etc. 'Pak' is often 'Americanized' to 'Park.' An *l (r)* in front of an *o* is pronounced *n* in Korean (Chinese Lao-tze > Sino-Korean Noja). Hence Mr. No T'aeu writes his name 'Roh' but of course calls himself 'No' (the *h* at the end is merely 'ornamental'). There are many family names that are written in special (and occasionally peculiar) ways by persons bearing them, e.g., Ch'oe – Choi or Choy, Cho – Joe, Im – Lim, Limb, Kim – Kimm, Kym, Sŏn'u – Sunoo, Sunwoo, U – Wu, Woo.

Around 1600 there were almost 300 family names; in 1930 only 256 of them were still in use.

The most common family names are Kim, Yi, Pak, Ch'oe, Chŏng and Cho (in modern Chinese these names read Chin, Li, P'o, Ts'ui, Cheng and Chao).

According to a survey made in 1930 there were at the time 858,239 families with the name Kim and 587,271 families with the name Yi. A well-known saying goes, 'If you throw a stone, you will hit the head of a Kim or an Yi.'

There are eight two-syllable family names, Chegal, Hwangbo, Namgung, Sagong, Sŏmun, Sŏn'u, Tokko and Tongbang.

Most families with the same name consider themselves to be related, but in actuality the number of patrilineal and exogamous clans is much greater than the number of family names. There are 1072 exogamous clans, i.e., four times as many as the total number of family names. For instance, there are 84 different clans with the name Kim. A Puan Kim is allowed to marry an Andong Kim (Puan and Andong are names of places), because they have different family origins *(pon)*. A Kangnŭng Kim may not marry a Kwangju Kim, however, because both families trace their family lines *(pon'gwan)* to the same clan, which was founded in the Silla era by Kim Alchi. The detailed genealogy of a family is found in the family register *(hojŏk),* in which marriages, births, divorces, etc. are recorded. Nowadays persons with the same family name are legally allowed to marry each other, if they are able to prove that their family origins are different. Tradition, however, often prevents such marriages.

A married woman retains her own family name. A Miss Kim who has married a Mr. Pak can therefore be addressed by a foreigner as either Mrs. Pak or Mrs. Kim.

Usually the complete name of a Korean consists of three syllables (i.e., three Chinese characters): Yi Ch'angsik, Song Yuhan. Persons with two-syllable family names therefore prefer one-syllable first names: Sagong Hyŏn.

Even in modern Korea 'generation names' are still quite common. In this case the members of one and the same generation of a family share one of the two characters of their given name. One may, e.g., find three brothers with the 'first names' T'aeho, Tuho and Kyŏmho. The syllable *ho* indicates that they belong to the same generation. The three sons of T'aeho are then called, e.g., Yŏng'ik, Yŏnggyun and Yŏnghwan, and his grandsons, Ŭnsik, Chŏngsik and Kŭngsik. The shared syllable in the 'generation name' thus alternates back and forth between the first and the second character.

In former times men also had a so-called 'courtesy name' or 'style' *(cha),* which they received on reaching maturity.

Scholars, writers and artists still use pseudonyms or pen names *(ho),* which usually consist of two syllables (characters). In the literature these *ho* can precede the complete name or be used instead of the 'first name' following the family name. The famous philosopher Yi I (1536-1584), e.g., had the *ho* Yulgok (Chestnut Valley). He is therefore referred to as Yulgok Yi I or Yi Yulgok (he had two other *ho*, by the way, Sŏktam and Ujae, while his style was Sukhŏn).

When they are ordained, Buddhist priests are given a Buddhist name *(pŏmmyŏng).*

After his death a person is given a posthumous name *(hwi),* which is written in calligraphy together with other data on a so-called spirit tablet *(wip'ae).* These spirit tablets, small, erect, rectangular wooden tablets, are kept in an ancestral shrine *(sadang)* at home.

In ancient Korea the daughters of noble families had personal names; daughters of commoners were numbered consecutively (e.g., Setchae, 'Number Three,' 'Third One') or had nicknames. Today all girls have 'real' names, in which we will often discover such Sino-Korean syllables as *ok* (jewel), *suk* (pure, virtuous), *sun* (obey) and *hŭi* (beautiful girl), e.g., Okhŭi (jade beauty) or Sunja (obedient child). *Kisaeng* (geishas) choose romantic pseudonyms such as Kukhyang (chrysanthemum fragrance) or Sŏnhong (fairy red).

Geographical names as well are almost exclusively Chinese (Sino-Korean). The most important exception is Seoul (pronounced like Eng. *soul*). We owe this rather peculiar spelling to nineteenth century French missionaries, who transcribed the Korean word *sŏul*, 'capital,' for French speaking persons as *se-oul*. This has led to a certain amount of confusion as to the correct pronunciation.

In 1413 Korea was divided into eight provinces. In 1896 the two northernmost ones and the three southernmost ones were each divided into two separate provinces, so that the peninsula now consists of thirteen provinces. The three undivided provinces are Hwanghae-do, Kyŏnggi-do and Kangwŏn-do (-do = province). The newly formed provinces were distinguished by the additional syllables *puk* (north) and *nam* (south), e.g., Chŏlla Pukto (the northern Chŏlla province) and Chŏlla Namdo (the southern Chŏlla province).

To make it easier for the reader to identify topographical terms, the following list contains the most important final syllables of geographical names appearing in this book:

-am	= cliff
-am	= hermitage
-chi	= pond
-chŏn	= hall
-ch'ŏn	= stream
-dae	= plateau
-dang	= hall, shrine
-do	= province
-do	= island
-gak	= pavilion
-gang	= river
-gok	= valley
-guk	= land, state
-gung	= palace
-ji	= pond
-jŏn	= hall
-kak	= pavilion
-kang	= river
-kok	= valley
-kuk	= land, state
-kung	= palace
-mun	= gate
-sa	= monastery, temple
-san	= mountain
-sŏng	= fortified city
-tae	= plateau
-tang	= hall, shrine
-t'ap	= pagoda
-to	= province
-to	= island

Homonyms with different meanings (-am, -am, -do, -do) are of course written with different Chinese characters.

Examples: Cheju-do = the island of Cheju; Pulguk-sa = Buddha Land Temple.

Paektu-san, Korea's highest mountain,
on the boundary between North Korea and
Manchuria

Geography, nature and landscape

Korea, a peninsula with an area of 220,741 square kilometers, has a population of more than 64 million persons (one third of them in the North and two thirds in the South). It is an extremely mountainous country and eighty percent of its territory is covered by hills and mountains, the highest of which is only 2,744 m above sea level. This highest mountain is Paektu-san (white-headed mountain), the source of the Yalu and the Tumen, the two rivers that form the natural boundary with Manchuria. Along the east coast the mountains are very steep. The landscape on the west and south coast is much gentler and there we find the country's other large rivers.

The most important mountain range is the T'aebaek Sanmaek, or 'Great White Mountain Range', which forms the backbone of the country. It extends from a point south of Wŏnsan on the northeast coast to an imaginary line between the cities of Taegu and Kyŏngju in the province of Kyŏngsang Pukto. Parts of the T'aebaek Range are famous for their scenic beauty, especially the Kŭmgang-san, 'Diamond Mountains', and the Sŏr'ak-san, 'Snow Peak Mountain(s)', in the east of the province of Kangwŏn-do. Such designations are – as is so often the case in Korea – somewhat confusing. Sŏr'ak-san, in 1967 classified as a national park, is used as the name of the highest mountain (1708 m) of the massif in question, as well as being the appellation for the entire area. Moreover, the Sŏr'ak-san may be (and is often) considered as the southern part of the Diamond Mountains, with the northern part situated in North Korea.

In this region are found many Buddhist temples, some of which are of a venerable age. Here it is worth mentioning that temples devoted to this religion are preferentially built on mountainsides or, barring this, at least on higher lying ground. An entrance gate, then, is also called *sanmun* (literally, 'mountain gate'), while *ponsan* ('mountain of origin') is the name given to the main temple of a Buddhist sect.

From the center of the T'aebaek Range, the Sobaek Sanmaek or 'Small Mountain Range' extends diagonally to the southwest, separating the Naktong River basin (see below) from the river basins located to the west.

The last mountain massif (also a national park) deserving mention here is the Chi[r]lisan (highest elevation 1915 m) in the Sobaek Range. This massif, partly located in Chŏlla Namdo and partly in Kyŏng-sang Namdo, is not only important as the seat of some very ancient Buddhist temples, but is also considered as an area holy to Korean shamanism.

The most important large rivers in the west of the country are the Taedong-gang (439 km), upon which lays the North Korean capital of P'yŏngyang, and the Han-gang (514 km) which flows through Seoul. In the southeast the Naktong-gang (525 km) deserves mention. Its several streams, originating from the T'aebaek Range, form a confluence that runs along Taegu towards the south and discharges into the sea west of Pusan. At the beginning of the Korean War, this river played a particular role as a final line of defense against the Communist advance.

Aside from the main peninsula that one thinks of as 'Korea', in fact Korean territory also encompasses over 3400 larger and smaller islands, of which only three will merit special note here.

The largest island is the sub-tropical Cheju-do, to which the second part of this chapter is devoted. Kanghwa-do, the fifth largest island, is located some 50 km to the west of Seoul and is divided from the mainland by the Yŏmha Strait. In the second of the first forty years of the Mongol Era (1231–1356), the Royal Court of Korea took up residence here, with the well defended Yŏmha Strait providing safety from the landbound Mongols.

The third island, Ullŭng-do, is of volcanic origin. Administratively belonging to Kyŏngsang Pukto province, it lies in the East Sea some 40 km off-coast. People here derive their income from fishing – squid, sea-cucumber, lobster and shellfish – with their catch primarily destined for the mainland.

A few miles east of Ullŭng-do we find the twin rocky islets of Tokto (called Takeshima in Japanese), not only of strategic importance, but also famous for the excellent quality of its seaweed, a beloved article of food in Korea and Japan. For more than four decades the possession of these two rocks has been a bone of contention between Korea and Japan. Another sensitive issue with regard to Korean national pride is the name of the sea where Ullŭng-do finds itself. On Western maps it is designated as the 'Sea of Japan', while the Koreans prefer to call it Tonghae, or 'East Sea', a name found in the oldest histories of the country. In ancient China, even the Yellow Sea was called the 'Eastern Sea'.

This digression on sea and islands, reminds us of a

Ch'ŏnji, 'Lake of Heaven', on the summit of Paektu-san

Ridge of basalt lava on Paektu-san

*Three of the most important rivers of north-east Asia
have their sources on Paektu-san:
the Yalu, the Tumen and (here) the Sang-hua (Sunggari)*

*Changsaek Waterfall is a popular tourist site
at the foot of Paektu-san*

Weather conditions are particularly changeable

Permafrost on a slope of the Paektu-san

*Virtually untouched nature in the northern part
of Korea (along the Manchurian border)*

charming description by Yi Ŭnsang (1903–1982) of *Oryuk-to*, 'Five or six islets': a seascape near Pusan consisting of uninhabited rocks, more of which are visible at low than at high tide. Yi Ŭnsang's small masterpiece consists of two *sijo* (see p. 88, l.), preceded by a short prose introduction:

> Oryuk-to…What a simple name! What a pure name! Of all place names in our country I like this one best. No Buddhist or Confucian thought is hidden in it; neither have scholars of the Chinese classics forcibly interpreted its meaning. What a good name it is – just indicating that five or six isles are meant!

> *Oryuk-to: there are five isles*
> *and – when I look again – there are six!*
> *Is the sky cloudy, then there are one or two;*
> *on a clear day there are five or six.*
> *When it is alternately cloudy and clear*
> *I do not know how many there are;*

> *When I look at them in my cups*
> *there seem to be ten or twenty isles.*
> *When there are fog-banks*
> *there is only a far, empty sea.*
> *And when I look today in the rain*
> *I have no idea at all.*

The climate of Korea is characterized by an abrupt transition from the continental to the maritime sphere. In winter land winds prevail, in summer sea winds. Consequently the differences in temperature are tremendous. The minimum temperatures range from minus 12–14° C in the south to minus 30–40° C in the north. Almost everywhere in the country the absolute maximum temperature is 35–40° C. Travelers who are accustomed to paddy rice agriculture in Southeast Asia will be surprised by the sight of frozen rice terraces in winter on Korea's mountain slopes. The nicest season is autumn with its gorgeous shades of color, the season in which 'the sky is high and the horses are fat.'

As a result of its climatic conditions, Korea's vegetation is very lush. We find many genera of conifers, 38 species of willow and 22 species of oak.

Korea's most famous plant, and for centuries her most important export product, is the ginseng *(Panax ginseng* C.A. Meyer, *Panax quinquefolius* L.; Sino-Korean: *insam)*. A cure-all, the ginseng root shows a marked resemblance to the form of the human body, and is especially popular as an aphrodisiac and rejuvenator. Wild ginseng is vastly preferred over the cultivated variety.

The *mugunghwa*, or 'inexhaustible flower' (rose of Sharon, *Hibiscus syriacus*), is Korea's national flower. The particularity of these white, violet, pink or red blossoms, is that they fall from the shrub after only one day in bloom, to then be subsequently replaced by new blossoms. Here, a parallel is drawn with the ever renewing spirit and power of Korea itself.

The many wooded mountains are home to a great variety of wild animals. The Manchurian tiger, which plays an important role in mythology, tradition, folktales and art, was exterminated during the Japanese colonial period (1910–1945). The bear has likewise disappeared from the landscape. Such animals as wild boar, lynx, fox, wildcat and deer still exist, however. Among the birds that we should mention are crane,

Halla-san (in the foreground a sacrificial altar)

Chŏngbang Waterfall. It plunges into the sea
not far from Sŏgwi-p'o (on the south coast of Cheju-do)

heron, pheasant, magpie, cuckoo, wild dove, wild goose, duck, crow and seagull. The seas surrounding the peninsula and the lakes and rivers of the interior abound in a multitude of fish species.

The typical Korean feeling of affinity to nature is aptly expressed in the following *sijo* by Sŏng Hun (1534–1598):

Wordless are the bluish green mountains,
formless are the running streams.
One cannot buy the clear breeze
and no one owns the full moon.
How wonderful it is to grow old among these
without suffering and free from worries!

Words, forms and possessions induce longing and hence suffering. In this poem we encounter true empathy with nature – in contrast to a sentimental love of its beauty or an intellectual definition of its phenomena.

In folk religion and art many plants, animals and birds have a symbolical meaning. The pine represents endurance and uprightness, bamboo is the symbol of longevity, endurance and loyalty. Peach blossoms signify transient erotic love. The tiger is the symbol of courage and strength. Crane and deer stand for longevity, one thousand years of life, whereas the tortoise, also a symbol of longevity, represents ten thousand years of life.

Since natural and cultural conditions on Cheju-do differ in many respects from those on the mainland, we will devote a special subsection to this island.

The southern part of Cheju-do

Cheju-do is a popular holiday resort

Cheju-do

Cheju-do (Quelpart) is a large island off the southern coast of Korea. It is 76 kilometers long from east to west and has a maximum width of 41 kilometers.

Rising from the center of the island is Halla-san, a mountain massif 1950 m high that is of volcanic origin (the last eruption occurred in 1007). Cheju-do is composed almost entirely of recent volcanic lavas, and it is primarily they that shape the surface forms of the island. The lava is extremely porous, hence a fresh water supply has been a serious problem on the island from time immemorial.

In ancient times the island was called T'amna. It was a small independent kingdom that was annexed by Koryŏ (918–1392) in 1105. In the *History of Koryŏ* (*Koryŏ-sa*, completed in the middle of the fifteenth century) we find the foundation myth of T'amna:

'In olden times the district of T'amna was inhabited by neither people nor animals. One day, however, three holes suddenly opened up at a place called Mohŭng at the foot of Halla-san and out of these holes three gods emerged. The name of the oldest was Yang'ŭlla, the second Koŭlla and the third Puŭlla. They climbed Halla-san and viewed the land around them. Nowhere was there a living being to be seen; only the wind rustled in the trees. The gods went to the beach every day, where they caught fish and clams, or to the mountains, where they gathered fruits. One day they caught sight of a large wooden chest with a purple sail floating across the sea toward the eastern coast. They pulled the chest onto land and opened it. In it they saw a man wearing a purple robe with a red belt and a stone box. When they opened the stone box, three girls dressed in azure robes appeared, and with them ponies, calves and seeds of the five grains. The escort accompanying these gifts spoke: 'I am an emissary from Japan. Our king has heard that you live all alone on this island and he sends you these young girls, begot by him, so that you may marry them and thus fulfill your great responsibility.' With these words the envoy mounted a cloud and disappeared. The three gods married the girls; the oldest god took the oldest girl as his wife, the middle one the middle girl and the youngest the youngest girl. They dug wells and laid out rice paddies. To stake off the areas where they were to live they shot arrows. The place where Yang'ŭlla lived

Cheju-do at sunrise

Wall-painting in a hotel lobby.
Azaleas at the crater lake of Paengnok on Mt. Halla
in the full bloom of spring

A Korean picnic

was called the First Capital, the place where Kŏŭlla live the Second Capital and the place where Puŭlla lived the Third Capital. They began to sow the five grains and raised the ponies and calves. Since then the island has developed continuously.'

The three holes are known as Samsŏnghyŏl (the holes of the three clans). They are located at some distance from the sacred mountain, Halla-san, in the vicinity of the capital, Cheju-si. Yang, Ko and Pu (-ŭlla means 'child') are still today the most common surnames on Cheju-do.

In 1273, during the Mongol domination of Korea (1231–1356), Cheju-do was incorporated into the Mongol Empire. For these new rulers the island played an important strategic role in their (unsuccessful) attempts to conquer Japan.

The Mongols started breeding horses on a large scale on Cheju-do, and traces of this can still be seen today. The leather headgear worn by old men in winter also dates to the Mongol period, as (probably) does the plow, which differs from the plow customarily used on the mainland.

In the night of August 15/16, 1653, the Dutch yacht 'De Sperwer' was wrecked off Cheju-do on the way from Formosa to Japan. Of the 64 crew members 36 reached land, where they were received quite well by the inhabitants, but did not receive permission to travel on to Japan. In the spring of 1654 they were brought to Seoul, where the king appointed them as his bodyguards. Two years later they fell out of favor and were banished to the southwestern province of Chŏlla, where they eked out a meager living. In the summer of 1666 Hendrik Hamel, the ship's secretary, and seven others were able to flee to Japan with a boat they had secretly bought. At the request of the Dutch on Deshima, (the small island in the bay of Nagasaki where the Netherlands East India Company had a trading post), the Japanese intervened with the Korean government on behalf of the eight shipwrecked Dutchmen still remaining in Korea, and in September 1668 seven of them arrived in Nagasaki.

In his *Journael*, published in Rotterdam in 1668, Hendrik Hamel recorded the adventures of the castaways. This was the first European book on Korea.

To complete this brief survey of the history of Cheju-do we must mention the tragic fact that in 1948 a Communist uprising began on the island and was not suppressed until near the end of the next year.

Twenty-seven thousand persons lost their lives, i.e., more than ten percent of the population at the time.

Cheju-do is a perfect example of how climate and topographical features influence the architecture, manners, customs and even the religious concepts of the inhabitants of a given area.

The island is jokingly referred to as Samda-do or Sammu-do. Samda-do means 'the island on which there is an overabundance of three things,' namely, wind, rocks and women; Sammu-do 'the island on which three things are lacking,' namely, thieves, beggars and fresh water.

To protect the houses from gusts and storms, the overhanging roofs are held together with nets made of straw ropes. Rocks are also often laid on the roof for the same purpose. Around isolated houses and graves the people build low walls of rocks gathered from the fields.

Whether there actually are too many women in Cheju-do is questionable, but a phenomenon that is certainly worth mentioning is the many *haenyŏ*, 'sea women,' i.e., diving women, who gather lobsters, oysters, clams, seaweed and other marine foodstuffs from the depths of the sea. In agriculture too the women on the island play a particularly active role.

Naturally the worship of wind and stone spirits is of great importance on Cheju-do. The first category includes Yŏngdŭng Halmang, 'Grandmother spirit light.' The deification of the winds that blow from Halla-san is known as Ilmun'gwan Paramun, 'Master wind governor.'

Halfway up the southern slope of Halla-san stand the so-called five hundred generals (Obaek Changgun), i.e., boulders that watch over and protect the mountain.

Another noteworthy feature are the many Tolmirŭk, 'stone Maitreyas,' also known as Torharŭbang, 'stone grandfathers,' hewn out of basalt, which grant wishes, such as for smooth childbearing, health and long life. These figures, which outwardly have nothing left in common with Maitreya, the future Buddha, are often erected in front or at the corners of important buildings, at sacred places and the like. Therefore we can assume that the original purpose of these statues was to define a particular area and to protect this area and its inhabitants from evil spirits that might cause harm and disease (cf. the *changsŭng* on the mainland).

Mongol ponies

A typical Cheju-do house.
The roof is held down by a net of straw ropes

A Tolmirŭk. Its shape still shows traces of the original
Bodhisattva figure

Ullŭng-do, a small volcanic island in the East Sea

　　　　　Oryuk-to, a jewel in the South Sea　　　　　*Entrance to the harbor of Pusan*

*Dawn at the South Sea creates
a picturesque and mysterious view*

A myriad of islands off the south coast
providing a rich harvest of seafood

Seaweed on Po'gil-to

Pusan. Fish market

Freshly caught cuttlefish drying in the sun

44

An island in the South Sea

Hong-do off the west coast.
Imposing, contorted rock formations line its coasts.

46

On the west coast,
fields run right down to the sea

Mountain ranges in the east
form the backbone of the country

Chŏndŭng-sa on Kanghwa-do
with view of the
Yellow sea

Autumn,
the most pleasant season of the Korean year

Naked rocks protude from the mountainside.
People often venerate strangely formed rocks
and believe in the presence of supernatural powers in stones,
trees and mountains

Crystal clear water streams over the rocks
after a heavy downpour

*Collection of shellfish in a sea-estuary
on the south coast*

*Irrigation of the rice paddies leads to the lakes
drying out in summer*

Andong in Kyŏngsang Pukto.
A region strong in Confucianism

Posŏng County in Chŏlla Namdo is known for its tea.
The county accounts for 80 percent of tea production
in Korea

Cultivation of toraji *or Chinese bell-flower*
(Platycodon grandiflorum) on a herb farm.
The roots are used as medicinal ingredients or as food

Rice cultivation is of prime importance in Korea

Lush vegetation in the vicinity of a temple

Kyeryong-san.
A tree serves as a natural shrine by the riverside

Cabbage is very important for making kimch'i
*(the spicy hot side-dish without which
no meal is complete)*

*Ginseng cultivation on Kanghwa-do.
For centuries ginseng (*Panax ginseng,
Sino-Korean insam)*, was Korea's most important export product.
Its root is a panacea for good health,
and is valued especially as an aphrodisiac
and rejuvenating tonic*

Dividing cut herbs into portions
in a traditional Korean pharmacy

Rice dish with ginseng

A streetside herb shop
shows the great variety of native products

Lotus pond in Naksan-sa.
Yangyang County, Kangwŏn-do.
The lotus is a symbol of purity

Pongjong-sa near Andong, Kyŏngsang Pukto.
Buddhist monk tending to dwarf trees

Pŏm'ŏ-sa in Tongnae County, Kyŏngsang Namdo.
In Buddhist temples as well, paintings of nature are often seen

58

The pond of Pong'ŭn-sa in Seoul.
The lotus preserves its purity in the mud

Bamboo at Pŏm'ŏ-sa, Kyŏngsang Namdo. Bamboo is
a symbol of longevity, endurance and loyalty

Seoul on the Han River

The Koreans

At the risk of being accused of oversimplification, we can state that the Koreans belong to the Tungusic subgroup of the Mongoloid race. Although we can assume that immigration from Southeast Asia also contributed to the formation of the Korean people, its influence is much less significant than in Japan.

The average Korean is larger than the Japanese. Koreans have short, broad heads and their faces tend to be flat with prominent cheekbones. The epicanthic ('Mongolian') fold is almost imperceptible in some cases, but it can be quite pronounced. Koreans' eyes are almost always brown (there are exceptions). Their skin color is yellowish to dark brown (especially in the countryside). Their hair is straight and black to bluish black, and they generally do not have much body hair.

Around five million Koreans live outside of the Korean peninsula. Most of them live in Manchuria (around two million) and Japan (more than 800,000). Koreans began immigrating to Hawaii to work on the sugar plantations in 1903. In April 1907 there were already 7000 Koreans in the Hawaiian islands. After the Korean War (1950–1953) more than one million Koreans emigrated to the United States. Owing to Stalin's curious population policies there are now more than 250,000 persons of Korean background in the five Central Asian republics. They refer to themselves as *Koryŏ-saram* (people from Koryŏ, i.e., Korea). Korean nurses have been working in Germany for years. Finally, we should mention the thousands of orphans who were adopted by persons from Western Europe and the United States in the 1970s and 1980s.

In this section we shall not bother ourselves with such questionable topics as racial or national psychology. We only wish to point out some typical Korean traits and customs that are particularly obvious to foreigners.

Koreans are very confident of themselves and proud: proud of their identity as Koreans and proud of their historical achievements, of such inventions as printing with movable iron and bronze type, their own alphabet, and the world's first armored ship. In the past few decades they have of course been proud of their industrial accomplishments, which are so well known in the West meanwhile that we need not go into them here.

Compared with their neighbors in East Asia Koreans are very individualistic, open and critical. Hence Europeans and Americans find them easy to get along with, but they are sometimes criticized by the Chinese and Japanese as being crude and ill-mannered.

Local pride is generally quite pronounced, and Koreans like to criticize and ridicule the traits and dialects of inhabitants of other provinces. There are even eight Sino-Korean phrases to characterize the inhabitants of each of the Eight Provinces, e.g., 'a wild tiger bursts out of the forest' (the inhabitants of P'yŏng-an province are impetuous); 'an old Buddha at the foot of a cliff' (the people in Kangwŏn province are too meek); 'slender willows in the spring wind' (people from Chŏlla are fickle).

Confucianism (cf. the chapter on Religion and Philosophy) had a tremendous influence on social and family life – unfortunately not always for the better. Even the ethical concepts of Buddhists and Christians are determined primarily by Confucian ideology. In Korean society each person has his superiors and his subordinates, and in general class consciousness is very pronounced. Consequently Koreans attach great importance to titles. To avoid unintentional offense, under some circumstances, e.g., in large offices, English terms of address, such as Mr. Kim or Miss Pak, are used. Koreans are particularly polite to elderly and/or scholarly persons. In the presence of their superiors (grandfather, father, professor, etc.) younger people do not dare to smoke or drink alcohol. It used to be customary to take off one's glasses in the presence of one's father; to approach one's father with dark glasses was of course unheard of!

Unedifying outgrowths of Confucianism are factionalism and nepotism – vices about which people prefer not to speak, but which the foreigner will observe in many aspects of social life.

Friendship is sacred and is expected to last a whole lifetime. Even when one lends a friend a considerable sum of money, it is considered bad taste to demand a receipt.

A concept to which much importance is attached is the 'family background.' It is of course particularly important when a marriage is being contracted. A good matchmaker will pay especial attention to the social compatibility of the two parties when he is searching for a suitable marriage partner. When young people in modern Korea fall in love and wish to get married, they almost always call on the services of a matchmaker, to reassure their parents.

Farmhouse with a straw roof

View of downtown Seoul.
In the background Pukhan-san

Mit'a-sa (Amit'a Temple)
surrounded by the rapidly expanding city of Seoul

The many chimneys serve for the floor-heating system (ondol)

The summer villa of the Taewŏn-gun,
father and regent of King Kojong (1864-1907)

The fireplace has always been the practical and spiritual center of every kitchen. In the background are large kettles for cooking rice

When an engagement or a marriage is contracted the horoscopes (borrowed from China) of the two partners play an important role. We mean here the so-called *p'alcha*, the 'eight [Chinese] characters,' two each for the year, month, day and hour of birth. These four pairs of characters, the 'four pillars,' are mysteriously connected with the five elements (fire, water, wood, metal and earth). By comparing the two horoscopes a fortune-teller can tell whether a particular marriage is advisable or not.

This brief discourse on marriage leads us to the topic of the status of women. Confucianism speaks of the *samjong*, the 'three obediences' of women: as a girl she should obey her father, as a wife her husband and as a widow her oldest son. Of course there have always been women who were not to be trifled with. Koreans say of a household with a henpecked husband: *amdalg-i unda*, 'the hen is crowing.'

Although the Korean man does not help his wife or any other woman into her coat (it is more likely to be vice versa), does not let her go first when leaving a room, etc., the modern Korean woman is most certainly not a pitiable creature. She manages her husband's salary (he gets an allowance) and has a decisive voice in her children's education. More and more married women have careers of their own. Secretaries, nurses, nursery school teachers, shop assistants and the like usually quit their jobs when they marry. Women professors, scientific personnel, doctors, etc. generally continue in their profession after marrying. In the government there are still comparatively few women.

There are two categories of women who were classified among the 'lowborn' in the Chosŏn period (1392–1910) but nevertheless played and continue to play an important role in society. They are the *mudang*, 'shamans' and the *kisaeng*, 'dancing girls.'

We will report on the *mudang* in the chapter on Religion and Philosophy. The origin of the *kisaeng* is supposed to date to the reign of King Chinhŭng (540–576). Since that time we find these girls at the royal court, not only as singers and dancers, but – in the Yi period – also as doctors and seamstresses. Because of the strict separation of the sexes doctors were not allowed to examine or treat the queen or princesses when they were ill – therefore the office of *kisaeng*-doctors. The *kisaeng*-seamstresses made and took care of the royal wardrobe.

In the provincial capitals there were inns maintained by the local authorities to entertain traveling officials. These inns had 'community *kisaeng*' who not only served and amused their guests, but also shared their beds on request.

In former times there were *kisaeng* schools. The most famous of them were in the northwestern province of P'yŏng'an-do. Pretty girls between the age of eight and ten were sold by their needy parents to these institutions. There they were instructed in good manners, music, singing, dancing and calligraphy.

Even today you may find *kisaeng* performing at banquets to entertain the guests. They play music, sing, dance, wait on the guests, use their chopsticks to stick choice tidbits into the mouth of their special guest, refill wine and beer glasses, light cigarettes, etc. Their entertainment is characterized by coquetry, humor and repartee. A guest at a *kisaeng* party should relax completely, which does not preclude the possibility that important political or business decisions may be made on such occasions.

No more than their Japanese colleagues, the *geisha*, are the *kisaeng* considered prostitutes. This certainly does not mean that they never go overboard, sexually speaking, but they decide whether they wish to bestow their favors on a person.

Since time immemorial the Koreans have loved dancing, music and drinking. In the oldest Chinese treatises on the inhabitants of the peninsula we can read that at certain festivities they 'came together, sang, danced and drank without stopping day and night.' Many Koreans are excellent dancers, musicians and singers. In Japan there are many singers of Korean background, both male and female, who use Japanese names.

A *kisaeng* party is the most extravagant way of entertaining friends and business connections, but the famous Korean hospitality can manifest itself in the many Korean, Chinese, Japanese and European restaurants and bars. A hearty appetite for drink is not frowned upon; it is more likely to be respected. Rash remarks made when drunk are not held against a person. Protestant Christians are always very puritanical and do not drink or smoke.

This chapter would be incomplete without a few remarks about the clothing and dwellings of the Koreans.

Since the discovery of the Koguryŏ murals (fourth

to sixth century), art can give us an idea of the development of Korean clothing through the centuries. What we know now as the traditional costume is derived from the Chinese dress of the Ming dynasty (1368–1644) and has since then been subject only to slight changes in fashion.

The materials used are cotton, hemp and silk. Men and women wear white trousers (*paji*). Over this women wear a skirt (*ch'ima*). It is actually only a large, ankle-length cloth, which is wrapped one and a half times around the body. On the upper part of the body both sexes wear a jacket (*chŏgori*). When he leaves the house, a man additionally puts on a coat (*turumagi*), which is usually gray in color. This clothing is often quilted in winter. It does not have any buttons, except for the vest, which was borrowed from the West. Pants and skirt are tied with ribbons. The jacket and the coat are held together by a bow on the right side of the chest. On their feet people wear white socks (*pŏsŏn*) made of cotton and boat-shaped rubber shoes ([*komu*]*sin*). In earlier times there were several types of cloth shoes with felt soles. In summer farmers like to wear straw sandals (*chipsin*). Dignified old gentlemen often wear a top hat (*kat*) made of woven bamboo or horsehair and coated with black lacquer. A type of Panama hat is also very popular.

Girls and young women often wear bright colors until they reach the age of thirty. After that white predominates, as it does for men.

Today many Koreans dress in American or European style, especially young people, of course.

The traditional houses in Korea are basically half-timber constructions. The main uprights rest on granite or other stone foundations dug into the earth. They and the beams connecting them are usually cut from red pine logs. The spaces in between are filled with wickerwork and plastered over with mud. The wooden latticework doors covered with paper have high thresholds and serve simultaneously as windows. In earlier times most of the houses had straw roofs, and only the wealthy had tile roofs. Today we see almost without exception tile roofs and, unfortunately, the much cheaper, ugly sheet iron roofs.

The houses universally have one story. The simplest floor plan is rectangular. More typical is a U or L shape. Two L-shaped buildings are often built in a rectangle around an inner courtyard (*madang*). In such large dwellings the ideal of 'three generations under one roof' is realized, i.e., here live a grandfather and grandmother with their oldest son and his wife and children.

At one end of the house lies the kitchen. It is almost always quite spacious. Flues leading from the two fireplaces in the stove heat the floors of the living rooms. The stone floors of the rooms are covered with oiled paper. The smoke comes out of a chimney at the other side of the house (in earlier times this was only an opening in the foundation). This floor heating system (*ondol*) appears to date to the beginning of the Christian era. Outside the living rooms is a veranda and there may additionally be a wooden hall (*maru*) that is not heated by the *ondol*. The veranda and the *maru* are protected by an overhanging roof. The number of living rooms depends on the affluence of the inhabitants. In the houses of the wealthy, e.g., the grandparents have their own rooms.

The toilet is outside. On farms it is often near the pigsty and on Cheju-do often over it.

Privacy is very important to Koreans. Wherever possible they surround their houses with a fence or a wall, to conceal them from immodest eyes.

Shoes are taken off before entering the house. The furnishings are very simple. People sit on the floor on round straw mats or cushions and eat or study at low tables. Furniture is limited to a couple of boxes or chests, which are often decorated with brass fittings or mother-of-pearl inlay. On the walls there will be only a few pictures or scrolls with calligraphy. Occasionally you may see a folding screen.

In the large cities of modern Korea many people live in apartment buildings. Private houses are often made of concrete and brick.

Pickling jars, especially for kimch'i, *spicy hot fermented vegetables.*
No meal is complete without kimch'i

Under-the-floor flues carry the heat from the kitchen fire
through the house and out through the chimney
on the opposite side

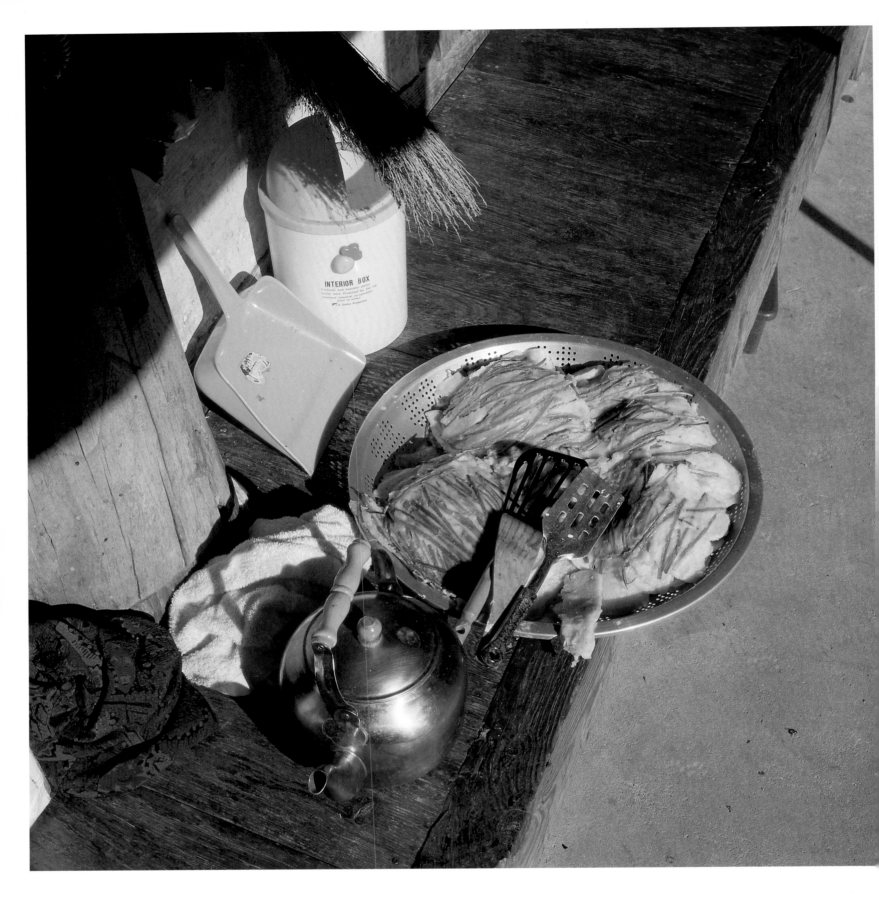

Vegetable pancakes are served at any time of day

Women preparing kimchi'i

A variety of tools and utensils are found in the traditional kitchen.
Songgwang-sa, Sŭngju County, Chŏlla Namdo

The entrance to a famous restaurant,
a popular meeting place

A waitress serving a guest

Taking pictures on a holiday outing

*Waitress in hanbok
at a traditional Korean
restaurant*

*Bridal couple in Chosŏn Dynasty
attire in front of the Myŏngnyun-dang
at Sŏnggyun-gwan University*

Father and son in a fishing village

School children on an excursion

A Buddhist monk applying the lotus-motif
to the ends of ceiling beams

74

An old Korean with a horsehair hat

Some tumuli around Kyŏngju.

Chronological chart

Mythology and Tradition

2333 B.C.	Founding of Chosŏn by Tan-gun
1122–194 B.C.	Kingdom of Ki-ja and his successors
57 B.C.	Founding of Silla
37 B.C.	Founding of Koguryŏ
18 B.C.	Founding of Paekche
42 A.D.	Founding of Kara

History

194–108 B.C.	Kingdom of Wi-man and his grandson
108 B.C.–313 A.D.	Period of Chinese commanderies
±100–120	Founding of Koguryŏ
±316	Founding of Paekche
±326	Founding of Silla
±326–663	Period of the Three Kingdoms
562	Silla annexes Kara
660–663	Fall of Paekche
661–668	Fall of Koguryŏ
668–892	Unified Silla
699–926	Parhae
892–936	Later Paekche
901–918	Later Koguryŏ
918–1392	Koryŏ
935	Fall of Silla
1231–1356	Mongol domination
1392–1910	Chosŏn dynasty
1592–1593	First Japanese invasion
1597–1598	Second Japanese invasion
1627–1637	Manchu invasion
1637–1876	Seclusion policy
1876	Opening of the country by Japan
1894–1895	Sino-Japanese War
1897	Korea becomes an empire
1904–1905	Russo-Japanese War
1905–1910	Korea as a Japanese protectorate
1910–1945	Korea as a Japanese colony
1919 (March 1)	Uprising and proclamation of Korean independence
1945	Partition of Korea into an American and a Soviet occupation zone
1948 (August 15)	Proclamation of the Republic of Korea
(September 9)	Founding of the Democratic People's Republic of Korea
1950–1953	Korean War (outbreak on June 25, 1950)
1953 (July 27)	Truce signed at P'anmunjŏm

The oldest observatory in East Asia, near Kyŏngju

History

Although Koreans like to speak of their five thousand year history, we shall refrain from going back that far into the past. Nor shall we expatiate on the details of the prehistoric period.

As tradition has it, Korean history begins in 2333 B.C. (i.e., in the middle of the Neolithic period), when a certain Tan-gun Wanggŏm, born of the union of a bear that had been transformed into a woman and the son of the creator, founded the country of Chosŏn (= Korea, cf. the section on Mythology). He established the seat of his government in P'yŏngyang, the present-day capital of North Korea.

The next important date is 1122 B.C. In this year a Chinese nobleman, the viscount of Chi, Chi-tze (Sino-Korean: Ki-ja), was invested by King Wu of the Chinese Chou dynasty with the fief of Chosŏn and supposedly arrived in Korea with 5000 retainers. He too made his capital in P'yŏngyang. He taught the people rites, justice, agriculture, sericulture, weaving, etc., and introduced the so-called Eight Injunctions (ethical maxims guiding relationships within the family and society).

Although Ki-ja's journey to Korea is mentioned in the first authentic Chinese historical work, *Shih-chi* (beginning of the first century B.C.), we cannot accept it as a proven historical fact. We can, however, assume that in the period before the second century B.C. there were adventurers and rebels from China who managed to acquire a special status among the tribes at the periphery of China proper and paved the way for Chinese culture. That such adventurers penetrated into northern Korea from Manchuria is not impossible, in fact it is quite likely.

During the bloody disorders after the downfall of the Ch'in dynasty (207 B.C.), exiles and rebel leaders fled from the northern regions into the wilderness along the lower reaches of the Yalu. Among them was a certain Wei Man (Sino-Korean: Wi Man) from Yen (in the vicinity of modern Peking/Beijing). At the beginning of the second century B.C. (i.e., during the Korean Bronze-Iron Age) he moved eastwards at the head of a band of several thousand men and proclaimed himself king of Chosŏn (i.e., northwestern Korea). He founded his capital southwest of modern P'yŏngyang. Wei Man recognized the suzerainty of the Former (or Western) Han dynasty (206 B.C.–8 A.D.). Several small states at the borders of his territory submitted to his rule, so that he soon became quite a

mighty sovereign, and his domain spread out on both sides of the Yalu. After ascending to the throne, his grandson and successor, Wei Yu-ch'ü (Sino-Korean: Wi Ugŏ), assumed a more independent position. He neglected his duties as a vassal, prevented contacts between the small neighboring countries and China and even undertook an expedition against the Liaotung peninsula. The consequence of this provocative behavior was that his kingdom and adjoining parts of the Korean peninsula were subdued in 108 B.C. by the sixth emperor of the Han dynasty, Wu-ti (r. 140–87). They were proclaimed a colony and divided into four so-called commanderies (Chinese: *chün*).

The Chinese colonial territory extended over almost the entire peninsula. Only the extreme south and the southwest were not annexed.

The most important commandery, Lo-lang (Sino-Korean: Nangnang), was in the northwest, with present-day P'yŏngyang as its center. This region already had something of a Chinese cultural tradition, and in this period, when large numbers of Chinese officials and merchants settled here, it became an important center of Chinese civilization in Korea. Numerous archaeological finds in this area show that the original inhabitants of the area must have been familiar with Chinese culture.

At this time several, primarily Tungusic tribes lived in Manchuria and on the Korean peninsula. The most important were the Puyŏ in Manchuria, the Okchŏ in the northeastern part of Korea proper and the Mahan, Pyŏnhan and Chinhan (known together as Samhan, the three Han tribes) in the southern part of the peninsula. It is conceivable that in the latter area we have to consider immigration from Southeast Asia.

During the course of the first century B.C. China's dominant position in Korea began to decline, and in the third century A.D. the Chinese colony was limited to the northwestern part of the peninsula. Meanwhile the Koguryŏ tribe (originally Cholbon Puyŏ) had branched off from the Puyŏ and formed a small, but powerful state centering around the present-day Manchurian border, probably around the beginning of the second century A.D. This state was also called Koguryŏ, a fact that is confirmed by the mythology (cf. the relevant chapter). In 313 this new kingdom, which owed its rise to its close contacts with Chinese culture, overthrew the remnants of Chinese colonial domination.

The Three Kingdoms

In the third decade of the fourth century we encounter the so-called Three Kingdoms *(Samguk)*. The territory of Koguryŏ, in the north, encompassed part of southern Manchuria and the Liaotung peninsula. In the southwest lay Paekche and in the southeast Silla, both of which developed out of confederations of the above mentioned Han tribes (that is, out of the Mahan and Chinhan). These kingdoms emerged as China disintegrated after the fall of the Later (Eastern) Han dynasty (25–221). They maintained political and cultural relationships with the various dynasties that ruled China simultaneously and successively from the third century to the end of the sixth century.

The founding dates given in traditional history are 57 B.C. for Silla, 37 B.C. for Koguryŏ and 18 B.C. for Paekche. This chronology, a consequence of Silla's later hegemony, is untenable.

Actually the term 'Period of the Three Kingdoms' (± 326–663) is not quite correct. In the extreme south, along the lower reaches of the Naktong-gang, between Paekche and Silla, there was a small region known as Kara that covered approximately the area formerly belonging to the Pyŏnhan. In 42 A.D. its first king, Suro, is said to have ascended the throne. It would be better to speak of the Kara or Kaya confederation and to assume that it came into being around the middle of the third century. The main territory of the confederation, Sanggara or Taegaya, is referred to as Mimana in the oldest Japanese historical works. Here a Japanese 'governorship' was founded, whose existence and functions are a controversial and 'sensitive' topic in modern Korean historiography. Although the Japanese interfered in the politics of the Three Kingdoms, they certainly did not have any imperialistic designs at the time. Their interests in the southern part of the peninsula were primarily cultural and economic in nature. In 562 Kara was annexed by Silla. Paekche was the only of the Three Kingdoms that had relatively good relationships with Japan.

Initially Koguryŏ was the most important and culturally most advanced of these countries. It owed its rise primarily to the fact that its territory already had a certain Chinese cultural tradition. The high level of its culture can be seen in the murals depicting dragons, tigers, plants, flowers, hunting and dancing scenes, the life of the deceased, etc. in stone tombs dating to the fourth to sixth centuries.

Chinese characters were also used at an early date. A stele, approx. 6.5 m tall, erected in 414 in honor of King Kwanggaet'o (r. 391–412) near the then capital of Koguryŏ, Kungnaesŏng (today Chi-an) in southern Manchuria, is covered on four sides with an inscription comprising more than 1800 Chinese characters.

In the last quarter of the fourth century Buddhism was introduced to Koguryŏ and Paekche and the study of Confucianism began in both countries. In 372 a Confucian Academy *(T'aehak)* was founded in the above mentioned Kungnaesŏng. Exactly 20 years later Buddhism became the state religion in Koguryŏ and Paekche; in Silla not until 528.

Naturally the Three Kingdoms did not always live side by side in peace and harmony, but it would be carrying things too far and is unnecessary to describe the many conflicts, intrigues and alliances.

For a long time, Silla played a subordinate role. Not until the end of the fifth century did it begin to flourish politically and culturally.

From time immemorial Silla society was rigorously divided according to the so-called *kolp'um* system. *Kol* means 'bone' and consequently 'blood relationship' and *p'um* means rank, social status. The highest *kol*, *sŏnggol* (*sŏng* = hallowed) or *chin'gol* (*chin* = true), comprised the clans Pak, Sŏk and Kim. Originally the rulers of Silla were elected in a Council of Nobles *(hwabaek)* by the heads of these three clans. Religious and political functions were combined; the rulers themselves were shamans and hence wore crowns that bore a striking resemblance to the shaman crowns of eastern Siberia. After the reign of Naemul Maripkan (356–402) the kingship was passed on within the Kim clan on a hereditary basis. Not until the beginning of the sixth century did the Silla rulers adopt the Chinese term for king, *wang*.

There were seventeen official ranks in Silla. According to tradition they were established in 32 A.D. The highest officials were also chosen from among the *sŏnggol*. In the first half of the sixth century a new civil service system patterned after the Chinese system was introduced. The names of the old ranks were, however, still used as honorary titles. Only in 682 was a National Confucian College *(Kukhak)* founded to train government officials on the model of the Chinese system.

The Three Kingdoms around 600 A.D.

Another typical Silla institution was the *hwarang* (literally: 'flower youth'). In the spring of 576 King Chinhŭng (r. 540–576) replaced the *wŏnhwa*, leaders of a group of more than 300 beautiful girls who performed (shamanist?) dances and the like, with the Hwarang, leaders of young men's leagues. The fact that the Hwarang, 15 to 16 year old youths from noble families, were selected for their beauty and decked out more or less like women (with powder and make-up), indicates their female origin. That young men took the place of the Wŏnhwa has been explained as the result of Chinese influence, but it is more likely that there is a connection here with the Chinhan's traditional youth initiation rites and youth leagues.

The Hwarang undertook hikes in the mountains, where they aspired to a communion with gods and spirits. Together with their disciples they devoted themselves to the cultivation of music, dance, magic and military exercises, which are closely related to the former in an archaic society. The Hwarang groups can be considered the elite of the Silla armed forces.

During the reign of King Chinp'yŏng (579–632) the Buddhist monk Wŏn'gwang (died 630) laid down his 'five secular injunctions' as the basis of the Hwarang-do, the 'Way of the Knight': (1) to serve the king with loyalty, (2) to serve one's parents with filiality, (3) to practice fidelity in friendship, (4) to never retreat in battle and (5) to refrain from wanton killing.

At the end of the sixth century, the emperors of the Sui dynasty (589–618) once again established a unified Chinese state. They pursued the goal of bringing all territories that had previously recognized Chinese suzerainty, such as Annam and northern Korea, under their control again. The second Sui emperor, Yang-ti (r. 605–617) sent three large expeditions against Koguryŏ (612, 613, 614), all of which failed.

Silla saw advantage in joining forces with China. After the rise of the T'ang dynasty (618–907) it attempted, with Chinese assistance, to annex its neighbors. The outcome of this collaboration was that Paekche was destroyed in the period 660–663 and Koguryo in 668, and Silla gained hegemony, first over part of the Korean peninsula and later over the entire peninsula.

The great hero on the Korean side in these wars was the Silla general Kim Yusin (595–673), whose entire life was given to the cause of the unification of the peninsula.

Although the Sui and T'ang emperors originally intended to incorporate Korea into a new empire, in 675 China withdraw out of Korea, partly perhaps because of the impending Tibetan threat, partly probably in order to rid itself of the obviously insolvable Korean question. The kings of Silla remained vassals of the T'ang and received their investiture from the T'ang emperors – a relationship that continued on in later centuries under other dynasties. The country was, however, for all practical purposes independent.

The Relationship Between China and Korea

China's attitude toward Korea developed from colonialism (108 B.C.–313 A.D., 612–614, 660–675) to a mild form of imperialism. Under the condition that the Koreans recognize their suzerainty, the Chinese emperors were willing to sanction the authority of the Korean kings. Until the end of the nineteenth century the Koreans, for their part, were always quite willing to 'render unto Caesar the things that are Caesar's.' To them it was an honor to zealously observe the principle of *sadae* (serving the great). The relations between China and its neighbors were governed by an extension of the Confucian concepts underlying East Asian family and social life. The neighboring countries looked up to China, the 'Middle Kingdom,' as a younger brother does to his older brother or like children to their father. More aptly put, this was the attitude that China deemed befitting. The interrelationships between the Middle Kingdom and its neighbors were dominated by *li* (Sino-Korean *ye*), etiquette. Within these relationships there were all kinds of gradations and nuances, varying from rather intensive supervision, as in Korea's case, to occasional contacts with countries like Burma. The ruler of a smaller country received nominally, and at times *de facto*, his investiture from the Chinese emperor; each year the Chinese calendar was sent to these countries for the dating of official documents. Chinese missions visited periodically, while the smaller countries sent embassies with tribute gifts to the Chinese court. The main significance of the latter missions was to recognize the superiority of China in the family of nations.

Schoolchildren on a trip to the tomb of the Silla general Kim Yusin (595-673) in the vicinity of Kyŏngju

P'osŏk-chŏng. 'Abalone Stone Pavilion'.
The garden of a pavilion (no longer extant)
dating from the ninth century. A ditch shaped
like an abalone (Haliotis tuberculata) is fed
by a spring. The king and his guests sat beside this ditch
and let their wine cups float on the water.
If a cup became lodged in front of one of the participants,
he was obliged to improvise a poem or empty the cup

The 'Green-blue Cloud Bridge' (lower part)
and the 'White Cloud Bridge' (upper part)
leading to the entrance to Pulguk-sa.
Pulguk-sa, 'Buddhaland Temple', was founded
around 535 and completed in 752

Pagoda in the style of the Silla period at Haein-sa,
a large temple founded in 802 on Kaya-san,
southwest of Taegu. Haein (Sanskrit: sāgara-mudrā),
'Ocean Seal', suggests the boundless expanse
of Buddha's contemplation: universal insight.

Pusŏk-sa, Yŏngju County, Kyŏngsang Pukto.
Inside the Chosa-dang, the Founder's Hall

84

The so-called Emille Bell (height 3.07 m, maximum diameter 2.27 m) which used to be at Pongdŏk-sa near Kyŏngju. It was cast in 771 to posthumously honor King Sŏngdŏk (702-736). The story goes that monks traversed the country collecting metal. Somewhere a poor widow jokingly said, 'I'm so poor, I can only contribute my daughter!' When the bell was cast, it made no sound. Then the monk remembered the woman. The metal was melted down again and the child was taken from its mother by force and thrown into the molten bronze.
This time the bell turned out quite well, but whenever it was struck, it mournfully cried: emi, emi, emille, *'Mama, Mama for your sake!'* *Today the bell is in the National Museum in Kyŏngju*

Unified Silla (668–892)

From a cultural point of view the first century of the Silla period (± 670-± 770) was the first Golden Age of Korean history.

This is clearly shown by the architecture and the sculptures that can still be admired in the vicinity of Kyŏngju, the former capital of Silla. Noteworthy are the architectonically interesting Pulguk-sa, 'Temple of the Buddha-land,' and the stone grotto temple Sŏkkur-am with its 27 reliefs, which are among the most beautiful in East Asia. Both of these structures date to the middle of the eighth century. One hundred years earlier, in the same area, the oldest still extant observatory in East Asia, Ch'ŏmsŏng-dae, 'observation tower for observing celestial bodies,' had been built. This observatory is about 9 m tall and shaped like a bottle. Its base and capital are, however, square. The positions of the stars were studied not with telescopes, but by observing their reflections in the water of a pond surrounding the tower.

In the past decades thousands upon thousands of pieces of jewelry, reliquaries, small Buddhist cult figures, urns, incense burners, rooftiles, etc., have been discovered in the tombs of the Silla kings and members of their families and the nobility. They give us an impressive picture of daily life, particularly that of the upper classes of society.

Merchants traveled with their ships to China, where they had several settlements. They transported Chinese and Indian goods to Korea and Japan and Japanese and Korean goods to the T'ang empire.

The population of Kyŏngju is supposed to have numbered eight to nine hundred thousand souls. Foreign merchants, even Arabs, are said to have resided in the city. The rich led a life of luxury; exotic animals and plants were held in gardens and parks. Cooking was no longer done on wood, but on charcoal.

In the field of literature certain developments also deserve our attention. For more than 1500 years Chinese was Korea's second language, and until the end of the nineteenth century every educated person was capable of reading and writing (not speaking) classical Chinese as if it were his own language. Nevertheless, it is not surprising that quite early people wished to write down songs in the Korean language. In the *Samguk yusa* (*Remnants of the Three Kingdoms*, compiled in 1285 by the Buddhist monk Iryŏn [1206–1289]), we find the texts of 14 *hyangga*, 'native songs,' (in contrast to Chinese poetry). These songs, which can be dated to the period between 579 and 879, are written with Chinese characters, some of which are used for their phonetic value and some logographically. By order of Queen Chinsŏng (r. 887–897) the *Samdae-mok (List [of Songs] of the Three Reigns)*, was compiled, an anthology containing more than one thousand *hyangga*, which unfortunately has been lost. Eleven *hyangga* have been preserved in the biography of the Buddhist monk Kyunyŏ (917–973). Stylistically they still belong to the Silla period, though not chronologically. Here follow two examples of *hyangga*, both contained in the *Samguk yusa* and composed by the monk Wŏlmyŏng (dates unknown). The first has a prose introduction, which we have shortened here:

On the first day of the fourth month of the nineteenth year of the reign of King Kyŏngdŏk (i.e., in the early summer of 760) two suns appeared in the sky and remained there for ten days. Because this was a very bad omen, the king had the monk Wŏlmyŏng sing a 'Song of Strewing Flowers' in honor of Buddha. Thereupon Wŏlmyŏng sang the *Tosol ka*, 'Song of Tuṣita Heaven' (the heaven in which Maitreya, the future Buddha lives):

Today, here, I am singing a Song of Strewing
*   Flowers –*
You, flowers who have been thus elected,
Serve – as I bid you in all sincerity –
The sublime Maitreya!

Later, when Wŏlmyŏng brought an offering in memory of his deceased younger sister, he sang:

Was it intolerable for you
That there is a Way of Birth and Death in this
*   world?*
Is that why you have disappeared
Without taking leave of me?
Like leaves blown off the same branch
By an early autumn wind,
But scattered in different places,
We do not know were we go.
As I am going to meet you again in Paradise,
I am biding that day, steeping myself
In the Teaching of the Buddha.

Paradise is the Western Paradise, where the Buddha Amitabha (Sino-Korean Amit'a) resides.

A Chinese poem by one of Silla's great scholars, Ch'oe Ch'iwŏn (857–?), entitled 'In the Rain on an Autumn Night' reads:

In the autumn wind I am singing sadly,
In the whole world I have few true friends...
Outside the midnight rain is drizzling,
In the lamplight my mind is roaming far, far away.

From the middle of the eighth century on the noble families vied with each other for the kingship and for power in the state. These feuds were associated with local uprisings and peasants' revolts, an increasingly corrupt government and a rapid decline of royal authority. These fights and revolts, combined with the founding of separate states – Later Paekche in the southwest in 892 and Later Koguryŏ north of modern Seoul in 901 – eventually led to the fall of Silla.

To make things complete we should mention that in 699 a former Koguryŏ general named Tae Choyŏng (died 719) founded a state on the ruins of Koguryŏ with the assistance of some of the former inhabitants of this northern state and the Malgal tribes. After 713 this state was known as Parhae (Chinese: P'ohai, Sino-Japanese: Bokkai), and it continued to exist until 926. Its territory comprised northeastern Korea and a large part of Manchuria.

The Koryŏ Period (936–1392)

In 918 Wang Kŏn (877–943), originally a supporter of Later Koguryŏ, founded the new kingdom of Koryŏ with Song'ak (modern Kaesŏng) as its capital. Eighteen years later he unified the whole peninsula again.

Although Koryŏ, from which our name Korea is derived, considered itself the successor to Koguryŏ, the core of its bureaucracy consisted of former aristocrats from Silla. Soon, however, the former class aristocracy was replaced by an official aristocracy. A civil service examination system modeled on the Chinese system was introduced in 958. Until they were abolished in 1894, these examinations were known by the name of *kwagŏ*. At the turn of the year 992–993 a Confucian university, *Kukchagam* (National Academy), was founded in the capital. Ch'oe Ch'ung (984–1068), the 'Confucius of Korea,' established the first private academy, which was followed by eleven similar educational institutions. Elementary education was provided by the *hyanghak*, 'regional schools.'

Around 1000 an army with 45,000 conscripts was established.

During the reign of King Munjong (1047–1083) a land reform was carried out. All land was nationalized and agricultural and forest land was allocated to the civil and military officials in accordance with their ranks. When an official died, his land became state property again. There were, however, also hereditary land allocations for particularly meritorious dignitaries and gifts of such 'temporary property,' which was also tax free, to members of the royal family and Buddhist monasteries. Although the land reform was introduced with the best of intentions, from the very beginning it contained the seeds of abuse and injustice. The farmers belonged to the land and led the life of slaves. They not only paid taxes in kind but were also subject to corvée labor and military duty.

The Wang dynasty strove to follow Chinese ideals and govern on a literary, i.e., Confucian basis. This endeavor was constantly thwarted, internally by politicizing Buddhist monks and several military feuds, externally by the Khitan, Jurchen and Mongols, who successively came to power in Manchuria.

Buddhism had remained the state religion, and high-ranking priests interfered in politics. Large monasteries sometimes had troops of monk-soldiers, who participated in all manner of conflicts. These conflicts arose primarily from rivalry between the aristocratic families (the descendents of [1] the former aristocracy of Silla, [2] Wang Kŏn's comrades-in-arms and [3] the officials who were ennobled in the early Koryŏ period). These aristocrats attempted to monopolize the high offices and marry members of the royal family, goals that led to diverse intrigues. In the second half of the twelfth century the two classes of officials, civil and military, opposed each other more and more fiercely and there were several struggles for power. In 1176 the first large peasant revolt broke out. It spread over the entire southern part of Korea and was not suppressed until 1193–1194.

The man who succeeded in pacifying the country was General Ch'oe Ch'unghŏn (1149–1219), who did away with all of his rivals, including members of his own family. The actual power in Koryŏ was in the

Some of the more than 80,000 wooden blocks used in printing the Tripiṭaka (first-half of the thirteenth century)

Celadon

A sophisticated, inlaid celadon medical jar preserved as National Treasure (nr. 646) in the Han-Dok Medico-Pharma Museum

hands of the Ch'oe clan for the next four generations (until 1258).

We indicated above that Koryŏ suffered greatly from invasions by the Khitan (993–1022) and Jurchen (end of the tenth century–1044). Particularly the Mongols threatened Koryŏ's existence as an independent state. In 1218 the country was forced to pay tribute to the Mongols. The recalcitrant Koreans broke off these relationships in 1224, and the Mongols retaliated with an expedition and even occupied Song'ak. After four further punitive expeditions they finally occupied the peninsula in 1258. In 1260 King Wŏnjong (r. 1260–1274) recognized Mongol suzerainty. The Korean kings were not deposed by the Mongols, but they were deprived of any real power. From 1274 on they were forced to marry Mongol princesses.

For almost a century Koryŏ remained part of the Mongol Empire. In 1274 and 1281 Korea served as the port of departure for the Mongols' (unsuccessful) expeditions against Japan.

A further source of distress for Koryŏ was Japanese pirates *(waegu)*. In the ninth century there had already been bands of pirates in Japan, but they did not begin to extend their raids to Korea, Formosa and the coasts of southern China until the thirteenth century, because they knew that Korean shipbuilding was unsurpassed in East Asia. Among them we find Chinese and Korean desperados, along with Japanese. Their raids culminated in the period between 1348 and 1351, but continued until the end of the sixteenth century. The coastal strips were depopulated and many 'displaced persons' joined these pirates.

The fall of Koryŏ was ultimately the result of struggles between parties within Koryŏ itself favoring the Mongols and those favoring the Chinese (in 1356 the Chinese captured Nanking, which had been in the hands of the Mongols; in 1368 the Ming dynasty was founded).

The most important product of Koryŏ art is – from the tenth century on – the exquisitely subtle grayish to bluish green celadon ware. The potters worked not only in the capital, but above all in the southwestern part of the peninsula (Chŏlla). Most of the pieces that still arouse our admiration today come from the graves of kings and high-ranking aristocrats. Characteristic of Korea are the so-called *sanggam* (inlaid) celadons (i.e., patterns incised and filled with white

slip), a technique invented in the middle of the twelfth century.

Of particular importance were the developments in the art of printing. Its antecendents go back to the Silla period, and the oldest prints in the world were found in a pagoda in the above mentioned Pulguk-sa. They are woodblock prints of *dhāraṇī* (Buddhist charms) produced between 704 and 751. During the Koryŏ period the *Tripiṭaka* (the Buddhist canon) was printed twice, once in the first half of the eleventh century (as a kind of charm to ward off the barbarian invasions from Manchuria), the second time between 1237 and 1251 on the island of Kanghwa. The 81,258 woodblocks used in the second printing are preserved at Haein-sa temple on Kaya-san (west of Taegu). Between 1957 and 1978 this work was reprinted in the Buddhist Tongguk University in Seoul.

Also on Kanghwa-do twenty-eight copies of the *Sangjŏng kogŭm yemun (Prescribed Ritual Texts of the Past and Present)*, a Confucian work in 50 sections, was printed with movable type made of iron between 1232 and 1241. Not until around 1400 did this procedure (with bronze movable type) come into general use. The invention of this technique – two centuries before Gutenberg – can certainly be considered Korea's greatest contribution to the civilization of East Asia (the Chinese used movable type made of clay or wood for printing at an earlier date).

Other works that appeared as woodblock prints were the *Samguk sagi (History of the Three Kingdoms)*, compiled under the supervision of the general-cum-statesman-cum-historian Kim Pusik (1075–1151) and completed in 1145, and the already mentioned *Samguk yusa*. The *Samguk sagi* is modeled after Chinese histories and contains four sections: annals of the rulers of the Three Kingdoms, chronological tables, treatises (on ceremonies, music, official clothing and geography) and biographies. Of the ten chapters of these biographies the first three are devoted to the great general Kim Yusin (cf. above). The *Samguk yusa* deals with mythology, traditions, legends and tales; it contains much valuable material on folk beliefs and early Buddhism in Korea. Both works are based on Korean sources that have been lost meanwhile and utilize a large amount of Chinese material.

The oldest collection of tales from the Koryŏ period is the *Silla su'i chŏn (Tales of the Extraordinary from Silla)* by Pak Illyŏng (died 1096). Only fragments of this book have been preserved in other works. In the twelfth century a new type of prose literature appeared: the *p'ae'gwan sosŏl*, 'Anecdotes.' These are fictitious miniature biographies and tales of 'human' deeds by animals or things. They are always laid in China, which has the advantage that the author could indirectly criticize grievances in Korean society. The greatest author in this genre was Yi Kyubo (1168–1241), who was also known as a poet.

Besides the *hyangga* there were three new genres of poetry in the Koryŏ period, of which we shall only mention the *sijo* here. A *sijo* consists as a rule of three lines:

a	3	4	//	3 (4)	4	syllables
b	3	4	//	3 (4)	4	syllables
c	3	5	//	4	3 (4)	syllables

Because each line has a caesura, *sijo* can best be translated as six-line poems.

An example follows, a *sijo* composed by Kil Chae (1353–1419) after the fall of Koryŏ on the occasion of a visit to Songdo:

On horseback I have returned to the place
That was the capital for five hundred years:
The mountains and rivers are the same as before,
But the great men are gone . . .
Alas! Was it nothing but a dream,
That time of prosperity and peace?

Until the Korean alphabet was invented (in the middle of the fifteenth century) *sijo* were passed down orally. In modern Korea they are still being composed.

Nostalgia for earlier times is heard in a Chinese poem by Yi Sung'in (1347–1406):

In the deep night a song from Silla –
Arresting our wine cups we listen together.
Its sounds transmit the old music,
Its effect is to make us think of those times.
The plaintive wind is rustling in the treetops
And a boundless aversion to the present grips our
*   hearts . . .*
Oh! To what purpose merit and wealth?

Another charming Chinese poem is that written by

Chŏng Tujŏn (died 1398) on returning from a visit to a hermit:

Autumn clouds are floating everywhere in the
*   distance,*
The mountains surrounding me are lonely and
*   deserted,*
Falling leaves are piling up without sound
And cover the earth like a red carpet.
By a brook I leave my horse behind
And ask someone the way home.
Have I forgotten
That I am a figure in a painting?

The Chosŏn Dynasty, First Period (1392–1592)

The Chosŏn or Yi dynasty, which ruled Korea from 1392 to 1910, was founded by the Koryŏ general Yi Sŏnggye (1335–1408). As its first king he was given the customary posthumous title T'aejo, 'Grand Progenitor.' Under him the country once again assumed the traditional name of Chosŏn, which was conferred anew by the Ming emperor. The new capital was Han'yang, also known as Hansŏng (= present-day Seoul).

Although T'aejo was a pious Buddhist, he was eminently aware of the dangers inherent in the excessive political influence of Buddhism and the power of the great monasteries. The policy he proclaimed was pursued by most of his successors. It is known as *ch'ŏkpul sung'yu*, 'driving out Buddhism and revering Confucianism.' During his reign (1392–1398) the tax exemptions granted to the Buddhist church were withdrawn. Under his successors measures were taken to regulate the property owned by temples. In 1424 all sects were reduced to the *Sŏnjong* (Contemplative Sect; Sŏn = Zen) and *Kyojong* (Textual Sect). Together they were allowed to have only 36 temples with a total of 3700 monks. Many Buddha statues were decapitated by iconoclasts and even the custom of drinking tea was abandoned, because it was considered a 'Buddhist' practice.

When we use the term Confucianism here and in the following we are referring to Neo-Confucianism (cf. the section 'Religions and Philosophy').

The highest organ of government was the State Council, which had three members. Its decisions were submitted to the king and after his approval they

A decapitated Buddha at the National Museum in Kyŏngju (a consequence of early Chosŏn Dynasty iconoclasm)

were transmitted to the Six Ministries for implementation. These Six Ministries were:

1 Personnel (high officials were appointed and dismissed by this ministry),
2 Finances (including population census),
3 Rites (including international relations),
4 Military Affairs (including production of military equipment, etc.),
5 Justice (simultaneously the supreme police authority) and
6 Public Works.

The provincial government was so constituted that each of the eight provinces had a governor appointed for a one-year term. He had jurisdiction over the various local magistrates, who were appointed for five-year terms.

The national defense was also reorganized. From 1464 on there were five Military Commands (in the Center, North, East, South and West). The troops that formed the core of these commands were professional military men. In addition commoners were drafted as soldiers. Moreover, each of the eight provinces had its own Army Command and Navy Command.

Naturally an extensive educational system was required to train the many officials. T'aejo founded a Confucian university, the *Sŏnggyun-gwan*, in the capital. The third king founded five Confucian academies, but his successor reduced the number to four (1445). In the countryside there were Confucian county schools (*hyanggyo*) and private village schools (*sŏdang*). State examinations, which were almost exclusively concerned with knowledge of the Chinese classics and Neo-Confucian commentaries, granted admission to the ardently coveted official positions. In China, where state examinations had existed from the time of the Sui dynasty, they were theoretically open to all; *de facto* only scions of the privileged classes could afford the considerable expenditure required for the many years of studies. In Korea only sons of officials could take part in the examinations. Sons of concubines were excluded.

The officials were known as *yangban*, 'the two orders,' a term that dated to the middle of the tenth century. It originally referred to the two classes of officials, the *tongban*, 'eastern order,' i.e., the civil officials, and *sŏban*, 'western order,' the military officials. *Yangban* can be translated as 'officials/literati'; today the term is used in the sense of 'gentleman.'

In the class hierarchy the *yangban* were followed by the 'middle people,' then farmers, artisans and merchants. The 'middle people,' *chung'in*, were the government clerks, scribes, translators, interpreters, technicians, doctors, artists, etc. Outside of the class hierarchy were slaves, actors, dancing girls *(kisaeng)*, shamans, pallbearers, butchers and shoemakers, who were called *ch'ŏn'in*, 'lowborn.' After about 1500 Buddhist monks were also included in this category.

The first century of the Yi period was Korea's second Golden Age. Particularly beneficial was the reign of King Sejong (1419–1450). In 1420 he established an academy, the *Chiphyŏn-jŏn* ('Hall of Assembled Worthies'), in which promising young scholars from all over the country joined him in studying various scientific topics. The members of this academy wrote many books on history, geography, medicine, politics, literature, etc. They also designed astronomical instruments, sundials and water clocks. In 1442, almost two centuries before they were invented by Benedetto Castelli, Sejong had rain gauges constructed and set up all over the country.

By far the most important event during Sejong's reign was the invention of the Korean alphabet (1444). After the usefulness of the new alphabet had been tested, it was officially promulgated in 1446 under the name of *hunmin chŏng'ŭm*, 'correct sounds to instruct the people.' This alphabet, the only scientifically constructed phonological alphabet in the world, originally consisted of 28 letters, 24 of which are still in use today. Though most of the *yangban* resisted the use of this simple writing and disparagingly called it *ŏnmun*, 'vulgar writing,' we nevertheless have a large number of poems, songs and novels written in this alphabet. For philosophical treatises and historical works classical Chinese continued to be the accepted mode of expression until the end of the nineteenth century. In modern Korea the term *ŏnmun* has fallen into disuse and been replaced by *han'gŭl*, 'great writing.'

The work in which *han'gŭl* was tried out, so to speak, is the *Songs of the Dragons Soaring to Heaven (Yong piŏch'ŏn ka)*, compiled by three scholars in 1445 by order of the king. This ode consists of 125 stanzas in the Korean language, each accompanied by a Chinese translation, likewise in the form of a poem. A translation of the first stanza reads:

Turtle made of granite, symbol of longevity (10,000 years of life). Its back represents the firmament, its belly the surface of the earth; hence it embodies the secrets of the universe

89

In the land east of the sea
Six dragons have flown up.
In everything they undertook
They were blessed by Heaven.
The sages of old
Were favored in the same way.

The six dragons are T'aejo, four of his ancestors and his fifth son, Yi Pangwŏn (= King T'aejong, r. 1401–1418), i.e., the direct ancestors of Sejong.

Among the historical works of this period, we should primarily mention the *Koryŏ sa (History of Koryŏ)*. This work, also modeled after Chinese histories, was printed in 1454.

Located in the capital was the *Ch'unch'u-gwan*, the official historiographical office, where all important events were recorded from day to day, as had been the case in the Koryŏ period. After the death of a king a temporary office was opened in which these records along with other government documents, e.g., royal decrees, were combined in the *True Annals (sillok)* of the government of the deceased king. Four identical copies of these *sillok* were prepared, and they were stored in four repositories specially prepared for this purpose in four different parts of the country. Hence the complete *sillok* have come down to us, despite wars and uprisings.

In literature Chŏng Ch'ŏl (pen name: Songgang, 1536–1593) stands out as one of Korea's greatest poets. More than seventy of his *sijo* are known. An example is:

By the roadside two stone Buddhas,
Naked and hungry, stand face to face.
Constantly they are assailed
By wind, rain, snow and frost.
Yet I look at them with envy,
For they do not know the pain of parting.

Chŏng Ch'ŏl was the grand master of the *kasa*, narrative poems that can on occasion reach a length of several hundred lines. Theoretically (there are many exceptions) each line consists of two groups with two four-syllable words each. A further characteristic is that they are written in parallel lines. The oldest *kasa* is 'A paean to spring' (*Sangch'un kok*) by Chŏng Kŭgin (1401–1481).

Secular architecture was of course more important than Buddhist architecture during the Chosŏn

dynasty. Soon after the founding of the dynasty two large palaces were built in the capital. The main palace, Kyŏngbok-kung, completed in 1405, is located at the foot of Pug'ak-san (north peak) and faces along the main axis of the city, which leads to the South Gate (Namdae-mun). To the east of the main palace, Ch'angdŏk-kung was built as a detached palace. Behind this palace lies the 'Secret Garden' (Piwŏn) with its marvellous lotus ponds, bridges, pavilions and other structures. During the Japanese invasion (1592–1598, cf. below) both palaces were destroyed, but they were later restored to their original state (Kyŏngbok Palace not until 1867).

In the arts we find interesting developments in ceramics and in lacquerware during the early Chosŏn period. At the court and among the *yangban* white porcelain modeled on Chinese patterns was much in demand. More popular among the people was the typical Korean *punch'ŏng* ware (*punch'ŏng* = powder blue-green), which came into fashion around the end of the fourteenth century and disappeared after the Japanese invasion (1592). In the art of lacquerware, cupboards, dressers, boxes for writing utensils, tables, plates, trays, bowls and vases were covered with lacquer and often with inlaid mother-of-pearl.

The first king of the Chosŏn dynasty, T'aejo, founded an academy of painting, *Tohwa-sŏ*, in the capital, and honorary titles such as 'national master' (*kuksu*) were bestowed upon exceptional artists. The greatest painters in the fifteenth century were An Kyŏn (1418–?), Kang Hŭian (1419–1464) and Yi Sangjwa (1465–?). An Kyŏn painted landscapes in the style of the Northern Sung dynasty ink and brush paintings of Kuo Hsi (eleventh century). His most famous painting is certainly *Mongyu towŏn to*, 'Dream of Strolling in the Peach Garden.' Kang Hŭian, a member of the literati, painted in the style of the Southern Sung dynasty and is also famous as a calligrapher. Yi Sangjwa was born in Chŏnju as a slave in a literati household. He was so talented that he was freed and given a position as one of the 'middle people' in the above mentioned academy. His great model was Ma Yüan (around 1200) of the Southern Sung. Popular themes for the amateur painters among the *yangban* were the 'four gentlemen' (*sa-gunja*): plum (courage), orchid (cultural refinement), chrysanthemum (integrity) and bamboo (creative prime of life).

Although at the beginning of the Chosŏn dynasty

Punch'ŏng

The 'Turtle Ship',
the world's first armored ship,
invented by Yi Sunsin

*Hyŏnch'ung-sa near Onyang,
a shrine dedicated to the memory
of Admiral Yi Sunsin*

Admiral Yi Sunsin (1545-1598)

the influence of Confucianism was very beneficial, in the long run its orthodoxy and conservative outlook prevented Korean civilization from developing. This conservativism bred the narrow-mindedness and self-sufficiency that proved to be so disastrous for both Korea and China in the nineteenth century. Another peculiar phenomenon is that in a country in which there was only one officially accepted philosophy, the *yangban* were involved in a large number of disputes as to how to interpret this philosophy. Their controversies at first led to the so-called 'literati purges' *(sahwa)* of 1498, 1504, 1519 and 1545. We shall not expound upon the reasons for these purges here, but it is obvious that in actuality they were pretenses for disposing of political and philosophical adversaries.

In the long run (from 1575 on) the contentious spirit of the *yangban* led to the formation of factions *(pungdang)*. The discord among Korean Confucianists continued to exist after Korea was incorporated into the Japanese Empire, and even now it has not completely disappeared.

The Chosŏn Dynasty, Second Period (1592–1920)

Relations between China and Korea were almost always harmonious in the first two centuries of the Chosŏn period and Korea was, according to Confucian views, properly cognizant of its position relative to the 'Middle Kingdom.'

Less congenial were the relations with Japan, which were again disturbed by Japanese pirates in the mid-sixteenth century. There were also constant problems associated with the three ports on the southeast coast that had been opened to Japanese trade.

Once the Japanese dictator Toyotomi Hideyoshi (1535–1598) had united his island country, he began to dream of world supremacy. The first step in this direction was to conquer China, whose territory he wished to divide up into fiefs for his vassals. From the Korean king he demanded free passage for his troops. The latter, highly outraged, denied this to him.

Beginning on May, 25, 1592, more than 150,000 Japanese soldiers landed in and around Pusan. Eighteen days later they had conquered Hansŏng (Seoul); in July P'yŏngyang fell; soon thereafter the Japanese reached the Yalu. China sent a relief army, which was

at first beaten by the Japanese. It took until 1593 before their attacks began to take effect. In the interior guerilla forces sprang into existence, consisting of peasants and Buddhist monks (!). They cut off the Japanese supplies. Meanwhile the Korean navy under Admiral Yi Sunsin (1545–1598), the inventor of the first armored ship in the world, had attacked the Japanese lines of communication, so that the Japanese were cut off from logistic support and from reinforcements and had to withdraw to the south.

An armistice was agreed upon (1593), and only a toehold in the extreme southeast remained under Japanese occupation. Protracted peace negotiations between the Chinese and the Japanese (the Koreans were not involved) broke down because of Hideyoshi's exorbitant demands, and in 1597 a second invasion began. This time the reaction of the united Chinese-Korean army was more successful, and the fighting was restricted in the main to the southeastern part of the peninsula (Kyŏngsang-do). In spite of an initial victory, the Japanese fleet again sustained heavy losses due to the activities of Yi Sunsin, who died a hero's death in battle. Shortly before he died (in August 1598) Hideyoshi ordered the cessation of hostilities.

The Korean campaign devastated almost the entire peninsula and decimated its population, without bringing Japan any tangible results.

In a Buddhist temple in Kyōto there is an earthen mound (*Mimizuka* = ear hill) with a monument on top of it in which the noses and ears of 38,000 (?) Chinese and Koreans who fell in battle are buried. More positive are the developments in Japanese ceramics. Among the Korean prisoners of war abducted to Kyūshū were entire potters' villages, and their involuntary resettlement gave Japanese ceramics a tremendous upswing. Here we need mention only the workshops of Arita, Chōsa and Kagoshima (and Hagi on Honshū). Around 1605 the Korean Yi Samp'yŏng discovered the first deposits of kaolin in the province of Hizen.

From 1604 on relations with Japan gradually normalized. In 1607 an official mission was sent to Japan. In 1609 a Japanese trading post *(Wae'gwan)* was again opened in Pusan, through which tobacco, red pepper and sweet potatoes reached Korea for the first time. The Daimyō (feudal lord) of Tsushima (a group of islands between Korea and Japan) continued, as formerly, to be the intermediary between the two countries in diplomatic and trade relationships. In addition to the mission sent in 1607 there were eleven further Korean missions to Japan, usually to felicitate a new Shōgun (at that time the actual bearer of state power in Japan) on his accession to office. These missions, which consisted of several hundred persons and made a great display of splendor, had not only a political but also a cultural significance.

With the exception of the periodical missions to and from China, Korea cut itself off from the outside world and consequently came to be known as the Hermit Kingdom.

Peace on the peninsula was not to last. In Manchuria a new power had emerged: the Manchu. Their leader had originally considered himself a vassal of the Ming, but in 1616 he felt strong enough to break off this relationship. As the Manchus began to invade Chinese territory, Korean troops came to the assistance of the Chinese. Thereupon the Manchus twice invaded Korea. In 1627 an agreement was reached establishing an older brother-younger brother relationship between the Manchus and Korea, while the Manchus recognized the father-son relationship between the Ming empire and Korea. In 1637 the king was forced to submit to the Manchu. Like the Mongols in an earlier era, the Manchu, who founded the Ch'ing dynasty in China in 1644, allowed the Korean kings to exercise power in their own country. In this manner they continued to maintain China's traditional stance toward Korea. The annual missions to Peking were kept up, but the tribute payments were considerably reduced. Although the Koreans fulfilled their responsibilities to the Manchus, until the eighteenth century their attitude remained 'hostile toward the barbarians.'

The controversies between the Confucian factions persisted. When a certain faction dominated the government, the adherents of the other factions retired to the countryside and plotted against those in power at the moment. The development of this cliquism parallels a constant decline of the official county schools (hyanggyo) and a very unhealthy numerical growth of private schools (sŏwŏn) founded by dissidents in the countryside. In the long run these sŏwŏn degenerated into institutions that propagated not only divergent philosophical views, but also oppositional political standpoints. At the begin-

ning of the eighteenth century there were 593 sŏwŏn! That this development greatly contributed to the internal weakening of Korea certainly does not need to be expounded here.

Despite its isolation, knowledge of the West and Western science trickled into Korea. The first such information was brought by the Korean missions that went to China at the beginning of the seventeenth century. The Italian Jesuit missionary, Matteo Ricci (1552–1610), who lived in China from 1582 until his death and had a good command of not only spoken Chinese, but also classical written Chinese, authored a book on Catholicism entitled, T'ien-chu shih-i (The True Meaning [of the Concept] of God). This book was introduced to Korea, and Yi Su'gwang (1563–1628) summarized the most important points. Information on Western geography and astronomy also reached Korea via China in this period.

Some remarks on the advance of Christianity into Korea are in place here. In 1784 the first Korean to have been baptized (in Peking), Yi Sŭnghun (1756–1801), returned to his home country and began to spread the Gospel as a layman. Eleven years later a Chinese missionary, Chou Wen-mu (1752–1801), followed him. In the first persecution of Christians (1801) he was put to death along with 300 Korean converts.

Let us return to history. During the reigns of King Yŏngjo (1725–1776) and his grandson, King Chŏngjo (1776–1800), we find a true, if only temporary, revival of the degenerate Korean culture. This renewed flourishing was nurtured especially by the so-called 'School of Pragmatic Learning' (Sirhak-p'a), which advocated inductive methods of scholarly research. This school had its basis in Neo-Confucianism, to be sure, but its representatives did not restrict their activites to the ethical reflections and metaphysical speculation of their predecessors. They proclaimed progressive social and economic theories and showed great interest in the natural sciences. Precursors of this school can be found as early as the second half of the sixteenth century and the beginning of the seventeenth century (the above mentioned Yi Su'gwang belonged to them), but their actual founder is considered to be Yu Hyŏngwŏn (1622–1673). The most important representative of Sirhak-p'a was Chŏng Yag'yŏng (1762–1836), an encyclopedist who concerned himself with political science, economics, historical geography, mechanics, medicine, musicology

Kyŏngbok Palace, originally built in 1405

The throne hall in Kyŏngbok Palace (Seoul)

In the inner-courtyard of Ch'anggyŏng Palace (Seoul)

The garden of Kyŏngbok Palace is a favorite location
for amateur painters

Taesŏng-jŏn, the 'Hall of Great Perfection,'
where the images of Confucius and his 72 disciples
are worshipped. In front of and inside this hall,
Confucius' birthday is celebrated on the 27th day
of the eighth month according to the lunar calendar.
It is part of the Sŏnggyun-gwan which was founded
in 1304 by An Hyang (1243-1306) as the national
academy for the study of Confucianism.
It still exists today as the Confucian University
of Seoul

Screen with typical 'literati painting'

The garden of Pyŏngsan sŏwŏn in Andong County,
Kyŏngsan Pukto, founded in 1613
and dedicated to the memory of the famous scholar
Yu Sŏngnyong (1542-1607)

Study in Tosan sŏwŏn, the private school of
the Neo-Confucian scholar Yi Hwang (1501-1570)

Third gate on the Mun'gyŏng Pass, Kyŏngsang Pukto.
During the Chosŏn period, Mun'gyŏng pass
was the only – and very dangerous – route
linking the Yŏngnam region to
the Seoul Kyŏnggi region

100

The Water Gate (Hwahong-mun) in Suwŏn.
Last quarter of the eighteenth century

A pagoda in the garden of the Chosŏn Hotel,
a replica of the Temple of Heaven in Peking, 1897

and phonetics. Christianity also aroused his interest. Two of his relatives had been converted to Catholicism and he himself wrote about the concept of God.

Among the exponents of 'Pragmatic Learning' we do not find blind admiration for China, but rudiments of a healthy nationalism. Unfortunately, *Sirhakp'a* did not continue to develop long enough, otherwise it could have played an important role in the modernization of Korea after the country was opened to intercourse with other nations at the end of the nineteenth century.

In literature the emergence of the genre of the novel around 1600 is of significance. In the beginning these novels were strongly influenced by Chinese models. There are novels written in Chinese about Chinese topics, novels written in Korean about Chinese topics and novels written in Korean about Korean topics. And there are novels written in two versions, Chinese and Korean, which can differ considerably from each other.

Hong Kiltong chŏn (The Story of Hong Kiltong) by Hŏ Kyun (1569–1618) is considered Korea's oldest novel. Precursor of the genre would be a better characterization. Hong Kiltong, son of a high-ranking official and a concubine, is excluded from an official career because of his birth. He becomes the head of a band of robbers and poses as the savior of the poor. The first true novel and the best in the true sense of the word is *Ku'unmong (The Cloud Dream of the Nine)* by Kim Manjung (1637–1692). The scene is set in China, and there is a Chinese version by Kim Ch'unt'aek (1670–1717). Here is a resumé of the contents: The monk Sŏngjin is sent to the dragon king with a message by the abbot of his monastery. In the palace of the dragon king he is received very cordially and for the first time in his life he drinks three glasses of wine. On the way home he stops to cool his scorching cheeks in a stream. When he starts to continue on his way he meets eight breathtakingly beautiful fairies on a bridge. They are the servants of a Taoist goddess, who have just paid a courtesy call to his abbot. He jokes and flirts with them until sundown. As punishment for their revolting behavior, the nine, Sŏngjin and the fairies, are banished to earth (i.e., to the China of the T'ang period) and reincarnated in various places. Under his new name, Yang Soyu, Sŏngjin has a distinguished career and enters into relationships with the eight former fairies

(with two of them as wives and the others as concubines). After many years the nine awake out of their dream (of their existence in banishment). Yang Soyu becomes aware of his identity as Sŏngjin. He becomes the successor to his former abbot, and the eight women become his disciples. Finally they all attain enlightenment and enter Amitabha's paradise.

Most of the novels are anonymous and undated. Based on the language in which they are written we can determine that the heyday of the classical novel was during the eighteenth century and the first decades of the nineteenth century. The supernatural plays a more or less important role in most of the novels.

Sim Ch'ŏng chŏn (The Story of Sim Ch'ŏng), which in its original form perhaps dates to the early eighteenth century, describes the adventures of a girl who sacrifices herself to restore her blind father's vision. Because the tale is suffused with Confucian morality, it was recommended as excellent reading for young girls.

Ch'unhyang chŏn (The Story of Ch'unhyang [Spring Fragrance]) may have its origin in a Korean classical opera *(ch'anggŭk)* from the eighteenth century. It describes the touching love story of Ch'unhyang, the daughter of a former *kisaeng* (dancing girl, geisha), and Yi Mongnyong, the son of a *yangban*. This best loved of Korean novels is noteworthy for the skilful characterization of the *dramatis personae*. It expresses vigorous resistance to the prevailing social system of the time.

The style of the classical novels (metric prose and abundant dialogues) is particularly suited to dramatization. Sin Chaehyo (1812–1884?) adapted several novels for performance as *p'ansori* ('one-man operas').

The work of Pak Chiwŏn (1737–1805), an exponent of 'Pragmatic Learning' who held that literature should serve practical purposes, is a genre of its own. Of his satirical novelettes – written in Chinese – we shall only mention *Yangban chŏn (Tale of a Yangban)* here.

In the dramatic arts we find, in addition to the already mentioned classical operas, masked dances and puppet theater. In both genres various population groups – *yangban*, Buddhist monks and shamans – are satirized primarily because of their morals and conduct.

In 1727 Kim Ch'ŏnt'aek (dates unknown, not to be

The pavilion of Kwanghal-lu near Namwŏn, where Ch'unhyang and her lover (the main character of the 'Story of Ch'unhyang [Spring Fragrance]') supposedly met for the first time.
Although the pavilion is a fanciful modern building, it is regarded as a manner of shrine

confused with the above mentioned Kim Ch'unt'aek!) compiled the first anthology of *sijo* and *kasa*, the *Ch'ŏnggu yŏng'ŏn (Enduring Poetry of the Green Hills [= Korea])*. Kim was originally a policemen, but gained fame as a poet and singer.

One of the most famous love songs among the *sijo*, the following is not from this collection (anonymous):

> *Now, what was love?*
> *What was it?*
> *Was it round? Was it square?*
> *Was it long? Was it short?*
> *Could one span it or measure it?*
> *It does not seem to be really long,*
> *Yet I do not know were it ends . . .*

Here follows another Chinese poem by the above mentioned scholar Chŏng Yag'yŏng, entitled 'A Memory of Songgyŏng' (Songgyŏng = Songdo, capital of Koryŏ):

> *Kingdoms and clans perished and perish*
> *In antiquity as in the present.*
> *Silently the bluish green mountains rise,*
> *Ignorantly the waters flow.*
> *Pinkish clouds are hanging above Sudong*
> *And a woodcutter's song is heard.*
> *Moonlight pervades the dilapidated terraces*
> *Where vegetation is wild and rank.*
> *In the western sky*
> *A lonesome bird wings away.*
> *Through the autumnal path by the temple*
> *A monk is pushing his way.*
> *Spending a while here*
> *With other travellers*
> *I hum a song about the sad events*
> *In a space of five hundred years.*

After the Japanese invasions Korean architecture was in a deplorable condition. In 1593 a former princely villa became the new royal palace under the name of Tŏksu-gung. In the following years it was considerably enlarged. King Chŏngjo (r.1776–1800) temporarily moved the capital to Suwŏn (south of Han'yang), because his father, who had been brutally murdered, had been buried in the vicinity of this city. Therefore we find in Suwŏn impressive fortifications and gates (among them the interesting water gate, *Hwahong-*

mun, with its seven arches). Finally, the many pavilions constructed all over the country in places with particularly beautiful scenery deserve our attention.

In the graphic arts, genre painting (Sino-Korean *p'ungsokhwa* = pictures of customs) flourished. The most important painters in this field are Kim Hongdo (1745–?), Kim Tŭksin (1754–1822) and Sin Yunbok (1758–?), whose charming impressions of daily life have come down to us as leaves of albums. It is probably correct to assert that the interest in the ways and mores of ordinary people shown in their pictures was inspired by 'Pragmatic Learning.'

On the 26th of January, 1836, the first European priest, Pierre Philibert Maubant, reached the capital of Korea. There he met Liu Fang-chi (Pacificus Liu or Ryou), a young Chinese priest, who had arrived in Korea three years earlier. Maubant determined that Liu was living an immoral life and acquiring money by dishonest means and therefore ordered him to return to Peking. In the next year Maubant was followed by his fellow countrymen, Jacques Honoré Chastan and Laurent Marie Joseph Imbert. The French missionaries entered Korea from Manchuria, crossing the frozen Yalu River in winter. To avoid being recognized as foreigners, they wore Korean mourning clothes, which cover the face. When preaching they used Chinese-Korean interpreters. The ordinary Koreans were of course particularly attracted by such concepts as the equality of all persons in the eyes of God and the coming of the Kingdom of God. In the summer of 1839 the second great persecution of Christians took place. The three French missionaries (Imbert had been appointed Bishop of Korea meanwhile) were tortured and decapitated, and large numbers of converts were also executed.

In the third great persecution of Christians (1866) nine French missionaries and thousands of Korean Christians died a martyr's death. This last persecution led Admiral Pierre Gustave Roze to undertake a punitive expedition. After two displays of naval force he appeared with seven warships along the island of Kanghwa and destroyed the town of Kanghwa. In the same year the American trading ship 'General Sherman' sailed up the Taedong River to P'yŏngyang, where it stranded. The crew of the ship was massacred by the local populace, and the ship was burned.

These just mentioned events occurred during the

regency of the Taewŏn'gun. When King Ch'ŏlchong (r. 1849–1864) passed away in 1864 without issue, Chaehwang, the 12-year-old second son of Yi Haŭng (1820–1898) was designated as his successor, King Kojong (1864–1907). Because of Kojong's youth his father became regent with the title of Taewŏn'gun (Prince of the Great Residence). Until his retirement (in 1873) the Taewŏn'gun continued to pursue an uncompromising isolation policy and was known as a ruthless opponent of Christianity. On the other side, he fought against corruption and took measures against the pernicious growth of private academies (sŏwŏn).

Even earlier – since 1797 – Europeans had attempted to explore the Korean coasts and/or establish trade relations. Here we shall only mention the appearance near Wŏnsan of the Russian frigate 'Pallada' under Admiral J.V. Putiatin (1853). As early as the eighteenth century some scholars of Pragmatic Learning were of the opinion that Korea could become a rich and important country only by developing trade relations with Japan and the West. They met with no response, however, and the isolation policy was retained.

Unquestionably with the intent of provoking an incident, in 1875 the Japanese warship Unyō sailed close to the coast of Kanghwa-do. It was fired upon by the Korean coastal defense, and this gave Japan a pretext for intervening in Korea. On February 26 of the next year the Treaty of Kanghwa was concluded. In it Japan recognized Korea's sovereignty and Korea committed itself to opening Pusan and two other ports to Japanese commerce. Between 1882 and 1887 a series of treaties of commerce and friendship were concluded with the Western powers, the first with the United States.

The last decades of the Chosŏn period by no means afford an encouraging picture. The country was weakened by corruption and party strife. China attempted to maintain its privileged position as suzerain. Russia and Japan, entirely aware of the strategic significance of the peninsula (a dagger pointed toward the heart of Japan, or a bridge toward the mainland), plotted and schemed against each other and against China. Japan was able to eliminate its rivals, one after the other.

In the Treaty of Shimonoseki, which ended the Sino-Japanese War (1894–1895), China and Japan recognized and guaranteed Korean independence. In 1897 Korea proclaimed itself an empire (Taehan Cheguk; the han is that of the protohistorical Han tribes). In the Treaty of Portsmouth (New Hampshire) at the end of the Russo-Japanese War (1904–1905), Japan's 'paramount political, military and economic interests in Korea' were officially recognized. On November, 17, 1905, the Korean cabinet was forced into an agreement that made the country a Japanese protectorate. In the following year, Itō Hirobumi (1841–1909) was appointed resident-general. Relations with foreign countries were handled by the Japanese Foreign Office.

Emperor Kojong, who had refused to sign the Protectorate Treaty, secretly sent three representatives to the Second Hague Peace Conference, to champion Korea's cause. The only result of this initiative was that the emperor was forced to abdicate in favor of his fainthearted son and that further measures were taken to subjugate the Korean people. For instance, the Korean army was disbanded. Many soldiers, however, evaded being disarmed and resisted the Japanese occupation until 1915 as ŭibyŏng, 'faithful fighters.'

In October 1909 Itō was shot to death by a Korean patriot named An Chunggŭn at the train station of Harbin in Manchuria (while en route to negotiations with the Russians). In August 1910 the second and last emperor, Sunjong, was deposed and Korea was incorporated into the Japanese empire under the name of Chōsen (the Sino-Japanese pronunciation of Chosŏn). Hansŏng (Seoul) was henceforth called Keijō (one of the Sino-Japanese words for 'capital').

Korea as a Japanese Colony (1910–1945)

On October 22, 1910, Korea was declared a Japanese Government-General and General Terauchi Masatake (1852–1919), Japan's former war minister, was appointed Governor-General (1910–1916).

After the annexation of Korea, Japan's stated goal was to assimilate and Japanize the Korean people; in reality the Koreans were treated as second-rate Japanese. Seen from an impartial point of view, the Government-General accomplished a great deal in the way of improving the infrastructure of the country. Agriculture and forestry, ports and the transportation network were modernized; schooling and health care were considerably expanded. All of these measures primarily benefited the Japanese economy, however. To intimidate the people, initially all Japan-

The small East Gate of Seoul in 1911.
Photo Dr. Norbert Weber O.S.B.,
Erzabt von St. Ottilien (1902-1931).
Courtesy of the Erzabtei St. Ottilien, Germany

Korean family in front of their house.
North Korea 1911.
Photo Dr. Norbert Weber O.S.B.
Courtesy of the Erzabtei St. Ottilien, Germany

ese officials, even school teachers, wore uniforms and swords.

Many Koreans emigrated, to the United States (especially Hawaii), Russia and China (especially Manchuria). Both the Russian Revolution and President Wilson's declaration on the self-determination of peoples (1917) naturally appealed greatly to Koreans.

In early 1919 the former emperor, Kojong, died. His funeral was taken as the occasion to prepare a nonviolent demonstration against the Japanese administration. On March first a Declaration of Independence *(tongnip sŏn'ŏn)* signed by 33 leading personalities (including 16 Christians) was read all over the country, followed by peaceful demonstrations. Because the Japanese military and regular police took ruthless action against this popular movement, in several cases the demonstrations degenerated into violence and public buildings were damaged or destroyed. To break the resistance, entire villages were burned down; more than two thousand people were wounded or killed, and tens of thousands arrested and imprisoned or – at best – brought to trial.

On April 17 of the same year a Provisional Government of the Republic of Korea *(Taehan Min'guk Imsi Chŏngbu)* was constituted in Shanghai with Dr. Syngman Rhee (Yi Sŭngman, 1875–1965), a personal friend of Woodrow Wilson's, as its first president. Attempts of this government to plead the Korean cause at the Versailles Peace Conference failed because of the opposition of the Japanese delegation.

The independence movement was not entirely unsuccessful, however. Governor-General Hasegawa Yoshimichi (1916–1919) was replaced by the more moderate Saitō Makoto (1919–1927). Koreans were permitted to participate in the administration, though to a limited degree, and some newspapers were allowed to appear in the Korean language. These measures should, however, also be viewed in the light of Korea's increasing economic importance for Japan, at the time particularly as a supplier of rice.

According to the Educational Ordinance for Chōsen of 1911 the main goal of education was to train loyal Japanese subjects. Under the influence of the new assimilation policy, the Educational Ordinance of 1923 decreed that all Korean schools were to be accorded equal status with those of Japan (proper!) and that in the schools no differences should be made between the two peoples.

The curriculum for the six grades of the primary schools for Koreans devoted 64 hours a week to the Japanese language and only 20 hours to the Korean language. Moreover, the textbooks for all other subjects were written in Japanese.

Even in 1939 every Japanese child in the appropriate age group living in Korea went to a primary school, but only one third of the Korean children.

In 1924 Keijō Imperial University (Keijō Teikoku Daigaku) was founded in Keijō (Seoul). A year later 89 Koreans and 232 Japanese studied here; in 1939, 206 Koreans and 350 Japanese. Additionally, during the colonial period a rather large number of Koreans studied at universities in Japan itself.

The period of relative liberality came to an end in 1936, when the military assumed power in Japan. In Korea Governor-General Ugaki Issei (1931–1936) was replaced by General Minami Jirō (1936–1942). Especially after the 'China Incident' (1937), i.e., the outbreak of war with China, heavy industry was developed in northern Korea. Apart from the puppet state of Manchukuo, Korea was Japan's most important supplier of foodstuffs and raw materials. After Japan's entrance into the Second World War (on December 7, 1941) the country was systematically plundered. Moreover, thousands of Koreans were forced to work in the war industry in Japan itself or recruited into the Imperial Army, generally in very subordinate positions. All Koreans were forced to take on Japanese names, and the use of the Korean language was prohibited.

In the period between 1895 and 1919 Korean literature was in a transitional period. The appearance of *Sŏyu kyŏnmun (Observations on a Journey to the West, 1895)* by Yu Kilchun (1856–1914) marks the beginning of a new literature. Eleven years later the journalist Yi Injik (1862–1916) published the first so-called new novel *(sin-sosŏl): Hyŏr-ŭi nu (Tears of Blood).* Not only the development of the plot of this novel was new, but also the language, because the author was the pioneer in the movement for writing in the vernacular *(ŏnmun ilch'i =* unification of the spoken and the written language).

The true rebirth of Korean literature was marked by the appearance of Ch'oe Namsŏn (1890–1957) and Yi Kwangsu (1892–1950?). In 1908 the former published the first *sinsi,* 'new poems,' i.e., *vers libres.* Credit goes to him for having broken with traditional prosody genres and introduced unconventional topics and ideas (for the time). In 1917 Yi Kwangsu published his first novel, *Mujŏng (The Heartless)*, the first really modern novel.

The bloodless resistance movement against the Japanese colonial administration was the expression of a renewed national consciousness. This new spirit manifested itself in literature as well. The Declaration of Independence, drafted by Ch'oe Namsŏn, is in itself a document of great literary significance.

Between 1919 and 1923 there appeared several literary magazines, in which young writers and poets, often inspired by various European literary trends, made their debut. In 1925 the KAPF (Korea Artista Proleta Federatio) was founded. As a reaction against class conflict-dominated literature, Ch'oe Namsŏn, Yi Kwangsu and other well-known authors organized a movement to further a genuine national literature *(kungmin munhak)*, whose birth, October 9, 1926, coincided with the 480th anniversary of the promulgation of *han'gŭl*. Owing to the activities of this group interest in *sijo* revived, in which genre Yi Pyŏnggi (1892–1968), Chŏng Inbo (1892–?) and Yi Ŭnsang (1903–1982) became the uncontested new masters.

The romantic poet Kim Sowŏl (1903–1934) held a special position. His most famous poem is called 'Azaleas' *(Chindallae)*:

If you are through with me
And will leave me,
I will let you go without a word.

On the Yaksan in Yŏngbyŏn
I will pick an armful of azaleas
and strew them were you go.

Please tread gently, step by step,
On those flowers
As you go your way.

If you are through with me
And will leave me,
I may die, but will show no tears.

(Yaksan is a mountain in the northwestern province of P'yŏng'an Pukto, which is famous for its azaleas. The poet came from this province.)

In 1931 the 'Society for the Study of Dramatic Art'

(Kŭg'yesul yŏn'gu-hoe) was founded. It propagated performances of European stage plays and contributed a great deal to the modernization of Korean dramatic arts. In the novels of the 1930s we also find new trends, of which Intellectualism *(chuji-juŭi)* deserves mention here. A representative of this school was the jurist Yu Chin'o (1906–1987), who in his novella 'Lecturer Kim and Professor T.' *(Kim kangsa-wa T. kyosu)* contrasted Korean and Japanese mentalities.

In the same period historical novels enjoyed general popularity, because they allowed the reader to dream himself away into the great periods of Korean history. The undisputed and very productive master of this genre was Yi Kwangsu.

We shall conclude this part of our presentation with an appropriate poem by the linguist Yang Chudong (1903–1977), written in the early 1930s, 'I am a son of this land':

The people of this land –
*Their minds are even whiter than their clothes.**
Wine and song they love as their wives . . .
I am a son of this land!

They are good and modest,
They have many dreams and smile a lot,
The people of this land,
But they have no strength and no blood . . .
Oh! I am a son of this land!

The people of this land –
Their minds are even poorer than their homes,
Peace and freedom they love as their brothers . . .
I am a son of this land!

They are lonely and forsaken
And their worries and tears are many,
The people of this land,
But they are living and breathing . . .
Oh! I am a son of this land!

Korea, 1945–1996

In the communiqué issued at the end of the Conference of Cairo by Roosevelt, Churchill and Chiang Kai-shek (November 22–26, 1943), it was proclaimed

* The predominant color of the national costume is white.

Bridal procession with palanquin. North Korea 1911.
Photo Dr. Norbert Weber O.S.B.
Courtesy of the Erzabtei St. Ottilien, Germany

Woman weaving. North Korea 1911.
Photo Dr. Norbert Weber O.S.B.
Courtesy of the Erzabtei St. Ottilien, Germany

that 'in due course Korea shall become free and independent.' At the conference in Yalta (February 4–11, 1945) the United States and the Soviet Union reached a secret agreement that should they operate together in Korea against Japan, the demarcation line between their armed forces would be the 38th parallel.

On August 8, 1945, the Soviet Union declared war on Japan, and two days later its troops marched into northern Korea. Precisely one month later, on September 8, American troops landed in Inch'ŏn, the port city near Seoul.

Liberation unfortunately did not bring the Koreans the fervently longed-for independence. On December 28, 1945, the foreign ministers of the United States, the Soviet Union and Great Britain agreed on a four-power trusteeship over Korea for the duration of five years. The agreement also provided for a Soviet-U.S. Joint Commission to prepare a provisional Korean government. This disappointing declaration was greeted in Korea by a wave of demonstrations and strikes.

In the following year the separate development of North and South Korea began. In February 1946, at a meeting of the people's committees and political parties in P'yŏngyang, an Interim People's Committee for North Korea was elected with Kim Il Sung (Kim Ilsŏng, Russian rendition Kim Irsen) as its chairman. Not much later a Representative Democratic Council was founded in the South with Syngman Rhee (Yi Sŭngman) as its head. Kim Il Sung (born in 1912) had been famous in the 1930s as a guerrilla leader against the Japanese in Manchuria. In March 1934 (when he was not yet 22 years old!) he became the commander in chief of the Korean Revolutionary People's Army. It has often been claimed that he is not the true Kim Ilsŏng, and that he wrongfully assumed the name of this famous partisan. Syngman Rhee had been the first president of the Provisional Government of the Republic of Korea (1919). From October 1933 on he was married to an Austrian wife, Franziska (later Francesca) Donner, and he devoted his entire life – though from abroad – to Korea's struggle for independence. Both gentlemen were well liked by their respective occupation forces, Kim as an orthodox Marxist yes-man, Rhee as an archconservative politician. Both of them later disappointed their patrons with their obstinacy.

The chairmen of the delegations to the above mentioned commission were the generals John R. Hodge and Terenti Shtykov. The primary goal of the meetings was to effect a reunification of North and South Korea. When they failed to bring any results and the Soviet Union refused an invitation by the American Secretary of State, George C. Marshall, to hold a four-power conference on the Korean question in Washington, D.C., in August 1947, the United States brought the question before the United Nations General Assembly.

On November 14, the General Assembly agreed in a resolution that before the end of March, 1948, general elections for a National Assembly should be held in all of Korea. A U.N. commission was formed to supervise the elections. The elections took place on May 10 of the following year, but only in the South, because the U.N. commission was denied entry to North Korea. On this occasion 198 delegates were elected to the National Assembly by 72% of the registered voters. Two districts on Cheju-do were not represented for a year because of Communist disturbances on the island. One hundred seats were reserved for the future representatives of North Korea. On July 17 a constitution was adopted, and on August 15 the Republic of Korea (ROK, Taehan Min'guk) was proclaimed with Syngman Rhee as its first president. The U.S.A. Military Government in Korea (USAMGIK) was disbanded on the same date, and the withdrawal of the occupation forces began.

On September 9 of the same year (1948) the Democratic People's Republic of Korea (DPRK, Chosŏn Minjujuŭi Inmin Konghwaguk) was proclaimed in P'yŏngyang with Kim Il Sung as premier.

According to a declaration by the Soviet Union, all Soviet occupation forces left Korea by the end of December 1948. The withdrawal of American troops was completed on June 27, 1949.

On June 25, 1950, North Korean troops crossed the 38th parallel with the intention of reuniting the peninsula by force of arms. That this attack came from the North is not surprising, because only there had a strong, modern and well disciplined army been built up with Russian assistance. The North also commanded battle-hardened veterans from the guerrilla fighting against the Japanese army in China and Manchuria, while the economic situation was initially much better there than in the South owing to the Japanese industrialization.

With the Russian representative absent from its consultations, the U.N. Security Council condemned North Korea as the aggressor and decided on an armed intervention.

Not until August 5 was the Communist advance contained at the so-called Taegu perimeter (i.e., along the Naktong River) in the southeastern part of the peninsula. With the landing of 70,000 American troops in Inch'ŏn behind the North Korean lines (September 15–16) the tide of war turned. On October 19 P'yŏngyang was taken and the advance toward the Yalu began. The lion's share of the foreign aid to the endangered Republic of Korea came from the United States, but fifteen other countries (Australia, Belgium, Canada, Columbia, Ethiopia, France, Great Britain, Greece, Luxemburg, the Netherlands, New Zealand, the Philippines, South Africa, Thailand and Turkey) sent detachments to Korea. The commander in chief, after July 8, 1950, was General Douglas MacArthur. Medical aid was granted by Denmark, India, Italy, Norway and Sweden.

From October 25 on 300,000 Red Chinese 'volunteers,' in actuality the divisions of the third and fourth armies under Chen Yi and Lin Piao, infiltrated into Korea. Within two months they, together with the North Korean army, reconquered the area north of the 38th parallel. 365,000 U.N. and South Korean troops then faced 485,000 Chinese and North Koreans (the Soviet Union granted only material assistance and moral support). The struggle lasted two and a half more years, but in effect the front fluctuated back and forth around the 38th parallel and a certain military balance of power was maintained. Meanwhile, because of his views favoring extending the war to Red China, MacArthur had been replaced as commander in chief on April 11, 1951, by General Matthew Ridgway.

On June 23, 1951, the Soviet ambassador to the U.N., Jakob Malik, proposed a cease-fire, a proposal that was accepted four days later by all countries involved in the war. On July 10 the first truce negotiations were held in Kaesŏng. They were continued on October 25 in P'anmunjŏm. It took until July 27, 1953, before the armistice agreement of P'anmunjŏm was signed.

In the Korean War 447,700 U.N. soldiers were killed (415,000 of them South Koreans) and 548,000 were wounded or missing in action (428,500 Kore-

ans). The number of Chinese killed, wounded or missing in action is estimated at 900,000 and of North Koreans at 520,000. These figures do not include the civilian casualties.

In the summer of 1952 Syngman Rhee was reelected to the office of president. Two years before the end of his second term of office, in September 1954, his Liberal Party attempted to push through an amendment to article 55 of the constitution (which had a two-term limitation on presidential tenure). Although the bill necessary for this was defeated by a bare majority, the government declared it accepted, 'because it was only a matter of a fraction of a vote.'

In the elections of May 15, 1956, Rhee received 205,253 votes in Seoul; Cho Bong Am (Cho Pong'am), a former Communist and head of the Progressive Party, 119,129 votes; and the Democrat Patrick Henry Shinicky (Sin Ikhŭi), 284,359 votes. Since Shinicky had died ten days earlier of a cerebral hemorrhage, however, in this case we can speak of an anti-Rhee demonstration. Moreover, to Rhee's dismay, John M. Chang (Chang Myŏn) of the Democratic Party had been elected Vice President (Rhee favored Lee Ki Poong as candidate, cf. below). In August of the same year Rhee had a monument erected in honor of himself on the side of Namsan (the South Mountain of Seoul). More than 24 m tall, the monument was topped by a statue of himself.

Alarmed by the 'writing on the wall' on the occasion of the elections of 1956, Rhee and his Liberal Party acted more and more despotically and brutally. On December 24, 1958, e.g., the opposition Assemblymen were locked out of the National Assembly and 22 laws were 'adopted' in their absence.

On March 15, 1960, the almost 85-year-old Rhee won the presidential elections for the fourth time, receiving 9.5 million of the more than 11 million votes. This result was already rather peculiar compared with 1956; stranger still was the election of the vice president. This time Rhee's bosom friend and loyal supporter Lee Ki Poong (Yi Ki-bung), a man detested all over Korea, ran away with a glorious victory over John M. Chang (8,300,000 to 1,800,000 votes).

In Masan, a medium-sized port town west of Pusan, riots broke out, and they were followed a week or so later by demonstrations of protest and disturbances in other parts of the country. Particularly worth mentioning are the demonstrations of thou-

P'anmunjŏm.
The room where negotiations are held

sands of students in Seoul. On April 26 Rhee finally resigned. Two days later Lee Ki Poong's oldest son, who had been the adopted son of the Rhees since 1957, shot his parents, his younger brother and himself. At the beginning of May Rhee went into exile in Hawaii, where he died five years later (on July 19, 1965).

On July 29, 1960 the first truly free elections were held, and on August 12, Posun Yun (Yun Posŏn, 1897–1990) became president. The new government distinguished itself by its incompetence, and on May 16, 1961, a putsch overthrew the government without any resistance worth mentioning. Lieutenant General Chang Do Young (Chang Toyŏng), who formed a junta with four others, became Head of the Military Revolution Council. Yun remained in office as president.

The strong man behind the coup was Major General Park Chung Hee (Pak Chŏnghŭi, 1917–1979), who had been second-in-command of the Second Army. In July 1961 he became Chairman of the Supreme Council for National Reconstruction. On May 19 of the following year Yun retired from the office of president and Park became interim president.

On December 17, 1963, Park became president. In May 1967 and in April 1971 he was reelected. Furthermore, on December 23, 1972 a new elective body called the National Council for Unification extended the presidential term of office to six years.

Of the events during Park's autocratic regime, the one we should mention first and foremost is the normalization treaty with Japan. It came into effect on December 18, 1965 (more than 14 years after negotiations had begun). At the beginning of 1966 Japan and the Republic of Korea exchanged ambassadors. Both countries profited from the normalization of their relationships, Korea because of Japanese investments and commercial credit, Japan because of the cheap labor in the Korean subcontracting industries.

To increase production five-year plans were promulgated, the first for the period from 1962 to 1966. An example: in 1962 in Ulsan, a town on the east coast north of Pusan, a large industrial complex was constructed. During the third Five-Year Plan (1972–1976) the largest shipyard in the world was built here, and in the summer of 1974 the first supertanker (250,000 t) built in Korea finished construction.

South Korea's economic development definitely took a vigorous upswing during Park's presidency. Between 1963 and 1974 the gross national product grew by an average of 10% per year.

The substantial improvements in the infrastructure also deserve our admiration. They were accomplished particularly by the *Saemaŭl undong* (New Village Movement). In the countryside new production techniques were introduced; the road network was improved and extended; the long neglected forestry management was overhauled; straw roofs, a traditional fire hazard, were forbidden and replaced by sheet-metal and tile roofs, etc. A spirit of neighborly help and cooperation was also fostered among the farmers.

In his foreign policy Park continued to take an inflexible anti-Communist stance. Between 1965 and 1973 he sent three divisions to South Vietnam to support the American forces (because in Korea only a truce agreement had been reached, there were still 40,000 American troops there).

On October 29, 1979, Park was shot to death by the head of the Korean Central Intelligence Agency (KCIA), Kim Chaegyu (1926–1980). Five years previously his wife had been killed in an earlier attempt on his life.

On December 6 Choi Kyu Hah (Ch'oe Kyuha) was elected president, but on the twelfth of the same month a group of officers led by Major General Chun Doo Hwan (Chŏn Tuhwan, born in 1931) seized control of the army and thus the actual power in the country. In August of the next year Chun Doo Hwan became President of the Republic of Korea. In the recent history of his country Chun has a particularly bad reputation because of his bloody repression of the demonstrations for more democracy and the associated unrest in Kwangju (May 18–27, 1980). Nonetheless, in August 1980 he became the new president.

In December 1987 the Vietnam veteran, General Roh Tae-woo (No T'aeu, born in 1932), was elected president, and on February 25, 1988, he took office. In the same year (from September 17 to October 2) the superbly organized Olympic Games were held in Seoul. An interesting result of the Olympics was the rapprochement between the Republic of Korea and the 'Socialist' countries, a process that was accelerated by the fall of the Berlin Wall and the dissolution of the Soviet Union. Particularly important was the development of trade relations with the People's Republic of China (since 1989) and the exchange of commercial agencies. In August 1992 diplomatic relations were established.

In the general elections of March 24, 1992, the Democratic Liberal Party (successor to the former Liberal Party) did not succeed in winning the absolute majority. It won 149 of the 299 seats in the National Assembly (the Democratic Party won 97, the new National Party for Unification 31, other parties 22).

On December 18, 1992, Kim Young Sam (Kim Yŏngsam, born in 1927) was elected president. In February of the following year, Roh stepped down as president and the Kim Young Sam administration began. In his inaugural address (February 25, 1993) President Kim pledged, among other things, to fight corruption in the public and private sectors. He also started a campaign 'to rectify the errors of history', the most spectacular consequence of which was the arrest of ex-Presidents Chun and Roh in November and December 1995. They were arrested on various charges concerning fraud and bribery, but they were mainly put on trial for their seizure of power in December 1979 and the ruthless suppression of the Kwangju demonstrations in May 1980.

In the latest general elections for the National Assembly (April 1996), the NKP, wich was previously named DLP but had changed its name to NKP (New Korean Party) in December 1995, gained 139 out of the 299 seats. Before the 15th National Assembly met for the first time on June 5th, the NKP succeeded in recruiting three Democratic Party members and nine independents, thus gaining a floor majority of 151.

At the risk of hearing that this survey of the history of Korea has 'the head of a dragon and the tail of a snake', we shall keep the last part of our remarks as brief as possible.

The head of state of North Korea – since October 1945 First Secretary of the Central Committee of the Korean Communist party, since 1948 premier of the Democratic People's Republic of Korea (DPRK), since 1950 commander-in-chief of the People's Army, since 1972 president – was, until recently, the 'great and beloved leader, Comrade Kim Il Sung', also known as the 'Red Sun of Mankind'. In Spring 1980 he designated his son, Kim Jong Il (Kim Chŏng'il, born in 1942), as his successor, an unprecedented event in the Communist world. From the beginning, personality cult and nepotism have been characteristic features of the North Korean regime.

On July 8, 1994, Kim Il Sung died of heart failure, but Kim Jong Il did not (and has not, as yet) become the new president of the DPRK and the new leader of the Communist Party. Although he is still referred to as the 'great and beloved leader', his only official function at present is that of chairman of the National Defense Committee, which automatically makes him commander-in-chief of the 1.2 million-man army. He rarely appears in public, and then he hardly speaks. It is said that he is observing the (Confucian) mourning period of three years for his father, but the veracity of this statement is open to doubt.

The most important ideals in the country are *chuch'e*, which could be freely translated as 'complete autarchy', and *ch'ŏllima*, 'Pegasus' (literally 'Thousand-*li*-horse', i.e. a horse that covers 1000 *li* = 400 km per day). According to the hagiographies of Kim Il Sung, the former concept dates to his time as a partisan. The Ch'ŏllima Movement developed in 1958 when part of the current Five-Year-Plan was fulfilled ahead of schedule. It is a movement in which groups of workers set themselves the goal of increasing production 'in a spirit of Socialist love for one's country'. In recent decades, however, the North Korean economy has lagged far behind that of South Korea. The condition of its industry is very poor. The same may be said with regard to its food supply situation. Since 1991 its annual shortage of grain has been estimated at two million tons. Moreover, the massive floods of the summer of 1995 wiped out much of its current crop. It secured 650,000 tons of grain from South Korea and Japan and imported 160,000 tons from Thailand, but this was far from sufficient. The prospects for this summer (we are writing this in July 1996) are also very bad, as new floods have again destroyed this year's harvest.

Several observers of North Korea fear that the DPRK will – in order to divert the attention of its population from these severe internal problems – undertake a new attempt to unify the peninsula by military means.

We will refrain from enumerating the various incidents instigated by North Korea in the demilitarized zone (DMZ) or in the seas surrounding the peninsula. These have been regularly brought up for discussion at the sessions of the armistice commission in P'anmunjŏm.

Nevertheless, there has been a certain degree of rapprochement, or at least a dialogue between North and South Korea in the past decade. On September 1, 1991, both republics were simultaneously admitted as members of the United Nations.

In conclusion of these remarks about recent Korean history, some attention should be given to problems associated with North Korea's nuclear development program.

On October 21, 1994, the U.S. Ambassador-at-large Robert L. Gallucci and the Vice Foreign Minister of the DPRK Kang Sok-ju (Kang Sŏkchu) signed a 'framework agreement' on the nuclear issue in Geneva.

This accord implied the immediate suspension of nuclear activities in the Yŏngbyŏn area (in the south of P'yŏng'an Pukto) and elsewhere, and the replacement of the North Korean graphite-moderated reactors and related facilities with light-water reactor power plants. Further, both sides would move toward full normalization of political and economic relations (including the opening of liaison offices in Washington and P'yŏngyang) and work together for peace and security on a nuclear-free Korean peninsula.

On March 9, 1995, an agreement on the establishment of the Korean Peninsula Energy Development Organization (KEDO) was signed in New York by representatives of Korea, Japan and the U.S.; it was to be responsible for supplying light-water reactors to the DPRK.

On June 13, 1995, a further agreement with regard to the solution of the North Korea nuclear issue was signed in Kuala Lumpur by representatives of the U.S. and the DPRK.

North Korea, however, shows few signs of cooperation with the International Atomic Energy Agency (IAEA), the authority and competence of which it recognizes only to a limited degree. In other respects, too, its behavior in military affairs invites constant suspicion; since the 1960s it has developed bacteriological weapons, and is exporting missiles as well as missile technology to such 'undesirable' countries as Iran, Syria, Libya, etc.

As regards a peace treaty, to be concluded after 43 (!) years of truce, the DPRK wants to negotiate with the U.S. alone, and is opposed to including South Korea and China in the peace talks.

President Kim Young Sam of the Republic of Korea and President Bill Clinton of USA proposed in a joint announcement, during their Summit Meeting, on 16 april 1996 in Cheju Island – South Korea, to convene a Four Party Meeting of representatives of the Republic of Korea, the Democratic People's Republic of Korea, the People's Republic of China and the United States, to foster a stable, permanent peace on the Korean Peninsula.

Lack of space keeps us from dealing with art and literature in the post-war period in the two Koreas, as we did for the earlier periods of Korean history. Naturally the visual arts and literature are dominated by Socialist Realism in the North. In the South we find tradition (paintings in traditional styles, celadon, *sijo*, etc.) along with the most varied modern trends. We refer the reader to the relevant literature on the subject. As a single exception we would like to quote a *sijo* written by the famous scholar Ch'oe Namsŏn when he returned to Seoul in February 1951 (the city had been evacuated by the Communists for the second time):

Of nine out of every ten houses
The doors are nailed up,
But into the hearts of men
More and bigger nails have been struck…
All these nails in doors and hearts.
I cannot get out of my mind.

A finely worked lock in Pŏmnyun temple

Munsu, riding a lion, symbolizes the Buddha's omniscience.
Magok-sa, Kongju County, Ch'ungchŏng Namdo.
The temple was founded in 640 by Chajang
who introduced monastic discipline (vinaya)
to Silla from China

Mythology

*T*he Tan-gun myth is generally considered to be the foundation myth of the entire Korean people. It is recorded – in classical Chinese – in the *Samguk yusa* (cf. p. 85). Translated in full it reads:

'In an old book it is written: in ancient times there lived Hwan'ung, the son of a concubine of Hwan'in. He thought often of the world below and wished to redeem mankind. His father knew of his thoughts. Down below on earth he saw Mount T'aebaek with its three prominent peaks. Through it he could bestow many blessings on mankind. Thereupon he gave his son the three heavenly seals and sent him down to rule the world. With 3000 retainers Hwan'ung descended to the peak of T'aebaek, took his seat under a holy *paktal* tree and named this place the Holy City. He is called the Heavenly King Hwan'ung. With the gods of wind, rain and the clouds he ruled over the grains, the duration of life, over diseases, punishments, good and evil – altogether he ruled over more than 360 things that affect mankind. And he guided the course of events in the world.

'At that time there were a bear and a tiger, who lived together in the same cave. They continuously prayed to the divine Hwan'ung to transform them into human beings. Thereupon the god gave them a bunch of supernatural mugwort and twenty pieces of garlic and said: 'if you eat this and do not behold the light of the sun for one hundred days, you will be transformed into human beings.' The bear and the tiger received these things and ate them. After she had avoided the sunlight for twenty-one days, the bear assumed the form of a woman; the tiger, however, was not able to keep out of the sun and therefore did not become a man. The bear-woman had no one to marry. Because she longed to conceive a child, she incessantly recited incantations at the foot of the *paktal* tree. Thereupon Hwan'ung changed his guise and married her. She conceived and bore a son, who was called Wanggŏm, the ruler of the *paktal* tree (= Tan-gun).

'This came to pass in the year of the tiger, the fiftieth year of the reign of Yao. Tan-gun founded his capital in P'yŏngyang and from this time on he called his country Chosŏn. Later he moved his capital to Paeg'ak Asadal, which is also known as Kunghol-san or Kŭmmi-dal. He ruled the country for a period of 1500 years.

'When King Wu of the (Chinese) Chou dynasty ascended the throne in the year of the hare (1122 B.C.), he invested the viscount of Chi with Chosŏn. Tan-gun then moved to Changdang-gyŏng. Later he returned, hid himself on Asadal and became a mountain god. He lived for 1908 years.'

Which old book is meant in the above text is unclear. Much of the *Samguk yusa* is based on older sources that have been lost.

Hwan'in is written with two Chinese characters that represent the approximate pronunciation rather than the meaning, in this case: Hanănim (today Hanŭnim/Hananim), i.e., The Lord of Heaven, God (< *hanăl,* modern *hanŭl,* Heaven, + *nim,* Lord). Of the two characters with which *Hwan'ung* is written, the first is used phonetically, the second semantically. Therefore one could read the name as Hanăsu or Hansu, 'Heavenly Man.'

Mount T'aebaek is Myohyang-san in Yŏngbyŏn-gun, P'yŏng'an Pukto.

The seals probably symbolize Hwan'ung's authority over the gods of the wind, rain and the clouds.

The *paktal* tree is a kind of birch *(Betula schmidtii* Regel*)*. This sacred tree should perhaps be viewed as the axis that connects Heaven, the world and the netherworld.

Tan-gun = the lord of the *paktal* tree. The Chinese character that expresses the Korean term *paktal,* is pronounced *tan* in Sino-Korean; *-gun (<kun)* = ruler, lord.

Yao is the name of a legendary model Chinese emperor. The year of the tiger (the tiger is one of the twelve Chinese signs of the zodiac: rat, ox, tiger, hare, etc.) corresponds to the year 2333 B.C., the 'beginning' of Korean history.

Paeg'ak Asadal should be identified with Kuwŏl-san in the province of Hwanghae-do.

For the viscount of Chi (Sino-Korean: Ki-ja) cf. the chapter on history.

In reality the Tan-gun myth is the foundation myth of one of the northern components of the Korean people, which lived in northern Korea and part of Manchuria. The Chinese called their territory Chaohsien (Sino-Korean: Chosŏn).

Bear worship, often combined with a belief in descent from a bear (totemism), is found in other parts of the northern Eurasian continent and in North America. In other respects as well the Tan-gun myth shows similarities to themes in the mythology of Siberia and Japan.

*This spot on Paektu-san looks like the place where
Hwan'ung, the Son of Heaven, descended
(one of the three peaks of T'aebaek-san)*

*The large bronze bell (chong or pŏmjong), cast in
1496, is inscribed with the reproduction
of a text by the famous poet Kim Suon (1409-1481),
calligraphed by Chŏng Nanjong (1433-1489).
In the Far East the dragon is not the gruesome monster
it is in Europe. It represents the male force
in the universe (yang), symbolizes imperial power,
and is associated with clouds and rain*

Another aspect of this mystical wood

*The grotto of the Sea Dragon on Cheju-do, provider of
protection from unwelcome invasion*

In the following we shall summarize other myths as well as we can. First the Kŭmwa myth:

'In a dream the Heavenly Emperor, Ch'ŏnje (= Hananim), appeared to Aranbul, a minister of King Haeburu of the Northern Puyŏ, and warned him that his descendants would found a new state in Haeburu's ancestral territory. On Aranbul's advice, the king moved his capital and henceforth named his country Eastern Puyŏ.

'On an excursion the childless Haeburu discovered a large stone that cried as he looked at it. The king ordered the stone turned over, and under it lay a small golden child shaped like a frog. Haeburu took the child with him to his palace and named it Kŭmwa (golden frog). Later he appointed him crown prince, and when he died, Kŭmwa succeeded him.'

Haeburu = Hăibŭl (sun radiance)? In the chapter on History, we saw that the tribe of the Koguryŏ had branched off of the Puyŏ. In Koguryŏ's foundation myth this circumstance is described as follows:

'One day King Kŭmwa discovered a girl on the bank of a river south of T'aebaek-san. When he asked who she was, she explained that she was the daughter of a river god (Habaek) and her name was Yuhwa (willow blossom). A young man who called himself Haemosu and claimed to be a son of the Heavenly Emperor had lured her to a house on the bank of the Yalu at the foot of Ungsin-san (bear spirit mountain). There Haemosu had raped her and then abandoned her. Her parents had therefore banned her to the place where Kŭmwa found her.

'His curiosity having been aroused by her story, Kŭmwa took her along to his palace and locked her in a room. Retreating into a corner, she tried to avoid being touched by the rays of the sun, but they followed her everywhere and struck her body. She conceived, and after a while she gave birth to a giant egg. King Kŭmwa threw the egg before the dogs and the pigs, but they did not eat it. He threw it onto the street, but the oxen and horses avoided it. He threw it onto the field, but the birds and beasts covered it and protected it. He wanted to cut it open, but he could not crack it. Being at his wit's end, he gave it back to Yuhwa, who wrapped it in a cloth and put it in a warm place. After a while the shell cracked, and a beautiful little boy appeared.

'He was a precocious child and at seven already a perfect marksman. Because in Puyŏ a good marksman was known as *chumong* he was given the name Chumong. Kŭmwa's seven sons and the ministers of Eastern Puyŏ were jealous of him, and Yuhwa consequently advised him to leave the country.

'With three loyal friends he reached the Ŏm river and explained to the water that he was a son of the Heavenly Emperor and a grandson of the river god. Thereupon the fish and the turtles formed a bridge, but when Chumong and his companions had crossed, they dispersed and his pursuers could not cross the river.

'When he reached a place named Cholbon-ju, he founded a city, his capital, and called his land Koguryŏ. Not only because of the first syllable of the name of his land, but also because he was a son of the Heavenly Emperor and his mother had been impregnated by the rays of the sun, he chose Ko (high) as his clan name. He ascended the throne as King Tongmyŏng.'

The three characters used phonetically for *Haemosu* could be read as *Hansu*, 'Heavenly Man'; Haemosu should then be identified with the Hwan'ung in the Tan-gun myth. The mountains mentioned here, T'aebaek-san and Ungsin-san, are also significant in this connection.

The egg, which looks like a lifeless thing but contains life, is a natural object of religious veneration. The egg can also be a symbol of the sun. From the above myth it is quite obvious that a sun cult existed in ancient Korea.

According to the official chronology King Tongmyŏng reigned from 37 to 19 B.C.

Because the [alleged] first king of Paekche, Onjo (traditional reign dates: 18 B.C.–28 A.D.) is supposed to have been a son of Chumong/Tongmyŏng, his kingdom does not have a foundation myth.

In the case of Silla we find three myths, however, and they are connected with the clan names Pak, Sŏk and Kim. The first myth is simultaneously the foundation myth of Silla:

'The chieftains of the six clans in the territory of Chinhan had gathered with their descendents on the bank of the stream Alch'ŏn to discuss the need to join forces and choose a virtuous and glorious ruler. Suddenly a strange lightning-like phenomenon fell from Heaven to a well at the foot of Yangsan, and those assembled saw a white horse kneeling and bowing there. When they approached the spot, they discovered a large purple egg. The horse, however, neighed and flew up to heaven. They broke open the egg and found in it a lovely little boy. When he was washed in a well, his body gave off a radiant glow. Birds and beasts danced in a row, heaven and earth shook, and the sun and the moon shone simultaneously bright and brilliant in the sky. Therefore they gave the lad the name Hyŏkkŏse (to dwell brightly in the world).

'Later a chicken-dragon appeared, which gave birth to a girl from its left flank. Her body and face were particularly lovely, but her lips were shaped like the beak of a hen. When the people bathed her in the stream north of Wŏlsŏng, the beak fell off. For this reason the stream is called Palch'ŏn (beak-shedding stream).

'At the foot of Namsan (South Mountain) the people built a palace for the two divine children and raised them there. Hyŏkkŏse was born from an egg. Because an egg resembles a gourd and the Chinhan called a gourd *pak*, he was given the clan name Pak. When the two divine children were thirteen years old, i.e., in the year of the rat, the first year of the (Chinese) *wu-feng* era, Hyŏkkŏse was installed as king and the girl became his consort. For sixty-one years he ruled over the country. Then he ascended to heaven. Seven days later his mortal remains fell to the earth. Then – as the people say – his queen also died. The people of the country wanted to bury them together, but a giant snake prevented them from doing so.'

Alch'ŏn is a stream near the later city of Kyŏngju.

Hyŏkkŏse is the Sino-Korean rendition of the three characters concerned; they could possibly be read in Korean as *pălgăn nwi*, 'bright or shining world.'

The chicken-dragon is an otherwise unknown type of dragon, but it is interpreted as a good omen. It is of course not surprising that a girl born of such a dragon should have a beak.

The *wu-feng* era (57–53 B.C.) is an era of the Former (Western) Han dynasty. According to the official chronology Hyŏkkŏse reigned from 57 B.C. to 4 A.D.

Regarding the origin of the clan name Sŏk we have the following myth:

'During the reign of King Namhae (traditional dates: (4–24 A.D.) a ship was preparing to anchor in the sea off the kingdom of Kara. Suro, the king of this country, and his subjects welcomed it with drums and shouts of joy and wanted to keep it in their country, but it sailed away and anchored in Ajin-p'o, east of Kyerim in Silla. An old woman discovered it and was surprised to see so many magpies gathered around it, crying. She climbed into a boat and rowed out to the ship to investigate it. Inside the boat she found a large chest which contained a handsome boy, seven treasures and some slaves.

'The old woman looked after the boy in her house for seven days. Only then did he tell the tale of his origin: 'I come from the Kingdom of the Dragon Castle, where twenty-eight dragon kings born of human wombs have reigned in succession. My father, King Hamdalp'a, became engaged to the daughter of the king of Chŏngnyŏ-guk and married her. She remained barren for a long time and prayed incessantly for a son. After seven years of marriage she brought forth a large egg. Since this was probably a bad omen, the people made a chest, put me (the egg) into it, together with the seven treasures and the slaves, and loaded it unto a ship, in the hope that I would reach a country in which I would feel happy and could found a kingdom. On the voyage I was accompanied and protected by a red dragon. And thus I arrived here.'

'The boy experienced many an adventure and grew up rapidly. King Namhae ascertained that he was an intelligent person and gave him his oldest daughter as his wife. When King Yuri (traditional reign dates: 24–57 (A.D.) died, he ascended the throne.

'Because he had once confiscated the house of another man with the lie, 'This was once my house,' his clan name was Sŏk (*sŏk* is Sino-Korean for 'former'). It is also said that since his box had been discovered because of the magpies, the 'bird' radical was dropped from the Chinese character for 'magpie,' leaving Sŏk as his clan name (cf. p. 22, g).

'Having been born by opening a box and breaking the shell of an egg, he was given the personal name of T'arhae (throwing off).

'He reigned for twenty-three years and died in the year of the hare (79 A.D.). The circumference of his skull was three feet two inches, the length of his skeleton nine feet seven inches. His teeth had grown together as if they were of one piece; his joints were connected like the links of a chain. The people shattered his skeleton and made a statue of it.'

Suro was the first king of Kara (cf. below).

Kyerim (chicken forest) is identical with Kyŏngju here.

In another version of this myth we read that not an old woman, but the village chieftain of Ajin-p'o and

One of the nude figures 'holding up' the eaves
at Chŏndŭng-sa on Kanghwa-do

Ceiling showing the heads of two dragons
in T'ongdo-sa, 'Universal Salvation Temple,'
in Yangsan County, Kyŏngsang Namdo
(halfway between Kyŏngju and Pusan).
Founded in 646. With its 65 buildings
it is the largest temple in Korea

Ceiling of Injŏng Hall decorated with phoenixes,
symbols of royalty and happiness
in Ch'anggyŏng Palace

A painting of Sansin with the pulloch'o,
herb of eternal youth

others opened the box and took out the egg. Suddenly magpies appeared and pecked open the egg. It contained a boy, who called himself T'arhae. He was entrusted to the care of an old woman in the village, who acted as his mother.

The seven treasures mentioned here are probably not the Buddhist *saptaratna*, but rather Shamanist cult objects, such as daggers, mirrors, bells, etc.

A red or yellow dragon rules the south.

For comments regarding the characters for 'former' and 'magpie' cf. the chapter on Language and writing system. (p. 20)

The thirteenth king of Silla, Mich'u (traditional reign dates: 262–284), was the first to belong to the Kim clan. He was a descendant of Kim Alchi, whose birth is connected with the following myth:

'On the fourth day of the eighth month of the year of the monkey, the third year of the (Chinese) *yung-p'ing* era (60 A.D.), a certain Mr. Ho set off at night for Sŏri near Wŏlsŏng. In Sirim (the forest of commencement) he saw a great light. A purple cloud reached down from heaven to the earth and in this cloud a golden box was hanging from a branch of a tree. At the foot of the tree a white hen was cackling.

'Mr. Ho reported this event to the king (i.e., King T'arhae), who went into the woods with him. When they opened the box, a small boy lay in it. The boy stood up – it was just like in the story of Hyŏkkŏse! For this reason they named the boy Alchi. Alchi is a word for 'small child' in our language.

'When the king returned to the palace with the baby in his arms, birds and beasts danced and ran merrily in a row along the road. The king chose an auspicious day and named Alchi crown prince. Later, however, he stepped aside in favor of P'asa and did not ascend the throne.

'Because he had come in a golden box, his clan name was Kim (gold). The Kim clan of Silla is descended from Alchi.'

There is a tradition according to which Hyŏkkŏse (cf. above), when he first opened his mouth, referred to himself as *alchi kŏsŏgan* (baby-ruler). *Alchi* should probably be read as *aji* (baby). In modern Korean *aji* is only used as a diminutive suffix. 'In our language,' because the text is written in Chinese.

That T'arhae designated Alchi as crown prince is an extraordinary piece of information, since the kingship was not hereditary in Silla. P'asa (tradition-

al reign dates 80–112) of the Pak clan was, however, the successor to T'arhae of the Sŏk clan.

Particularly complicated is the foundation myth of the Kara or Kaya confederation, of which we again can only trace the main outlines:

'In the year of the tiger (here 42 A.D.) a strange voice resounded from the summit of Kuji, calling the nine chieftains of this area to welcome their great king.

'A purple rope came down from heaven. Fastened to its lower end was a golden box wrapped in a red cloth. In the box were six golden eggs, which shone like the sun. After the people had bowed many times, they wrapped the box back up in the cloth and brought it to the house of the *adogan*, one of the chieftains.

'At dawn on the thirteenth day after this event they again gathered and opened the box. The six eggs had been transformed into boys with noble countenances. They grew rapidly and after ten to twelve days they had reached a height of nine feet. Their physiognomy was also out of the ordinary: their countenances were like those of dragons, their eyebrows were of eight colors, and their eyes had double pupils.

'The firstborn became the first king; his taboo name was Suro. The country was called Great Kara or Kaya-guk, because it is an area in the confederation of the Six Kaya. The other five divine persons became the rulers of the five other Kayas.'

(There then follows a report of the visit of T'arhae to Kara [cf. above]. With the intention of taking the throne away from Suro, he enters into a contest in magic skills with him, but loses and takes his leave.)

'When the nine chieftains urged the king to marry the most virtuous virgin among their daughters, he refused with the words: 'That We descended here is a decree of heaven. To find a wife for Us and make her Our consort will also be a decree of Heaven. Do not be concerned!'

'Indeed, a ship with a purple sail and a red flag suddenly appeared from the southwestern corner of the sea. On board was a beautiful princess, who only consented to come to the palace after some hesitation and a sacrifice to the Mountain Spirit.

'When Suro and she were alone in the bedroom, she explained that she was a princess from Ayut'a-guk; her name was Hŏ Hwang'ok and she was sixteen years old. Following a command from the Heavenly Emperor her parents sent her to Kara to marry Suro.

'Only after many years of marriage did Hwang'ok

The mountain spirit (Sansin) *with his tiger*

Kyŏngbok Palace. Haet'ae *on the Yŏngje Bridge.*
It was common practice to install a haet'ae,
a mythical animal warding off fire nearby a bridge
or a building

122

bear the crown prince, Kŏdŭng. In the year of the snake (in this case 189) she died at the age of 157. The king's grief was immense. Ten years later, in the year of the hare (199) he died at the age of 158.'

A dragon countenance is the face of a king or emperor.

In the tale of T'arhae (the foundation myth of the clan name Sŏk) we read that he sailed past Kara as an egg or a small boy, depending on the version. According to the interpolation here in Kara he was already three feet tall (one third the size of Suro).

Ayut'a is the Korean rendition of (Sanskrit) Ayodhyā, the capital of the kingdom of Kosala (modern Oudh). Ayodhyā is already mentioned in the Indian epic Rāmāyaṇa (composed between the third century B.C. and the third century A.D.). It is of course very implausible that a princess with a Chinese name (Hŏ Hwang'ok = Hsü Huang-yü) should have come to Korea from an Indian kingdom in the first century A.D. (the ship appeared, by the way, from the southwest).

Suro's clan name and that of his brothers was again Kim (gold), because they were born from golden eggs.

Kŏdŭng would have ruled over Kara from 199 to 253 as King To.

Since traditions involving persons born from eggs are found among the ethnic minorities in southern China and Indochina, one could perhaps speak of Southeast Asian influences on Korean mythology in this context.

Korea's stock of myths has certainly not been exhaustively described here, but we are forced to limit ourselves. We would, however, like to refer the reader to the foundation myth of T'amna/Cheju-do (p. 35).

A beast engulfing fire, mostly found at the entrance of a building. It resembles an elephant, but also possesses many features making it worthy of veneration as a deity. Kwanghal- lu, Namwŏn

*Beautifully carved and painted wall panels
inside Chikchi-sa, Kŭmnŭng County, Kyŏngsang Pukto*

124

Often these panels reach a length of several meters

*Mythical figures on a chimney
in Kyŏngbok Palace*

*Aries, one of the twelve signs of the zodiac, guarding
the tomb of General Kim Yusin (595-673)*

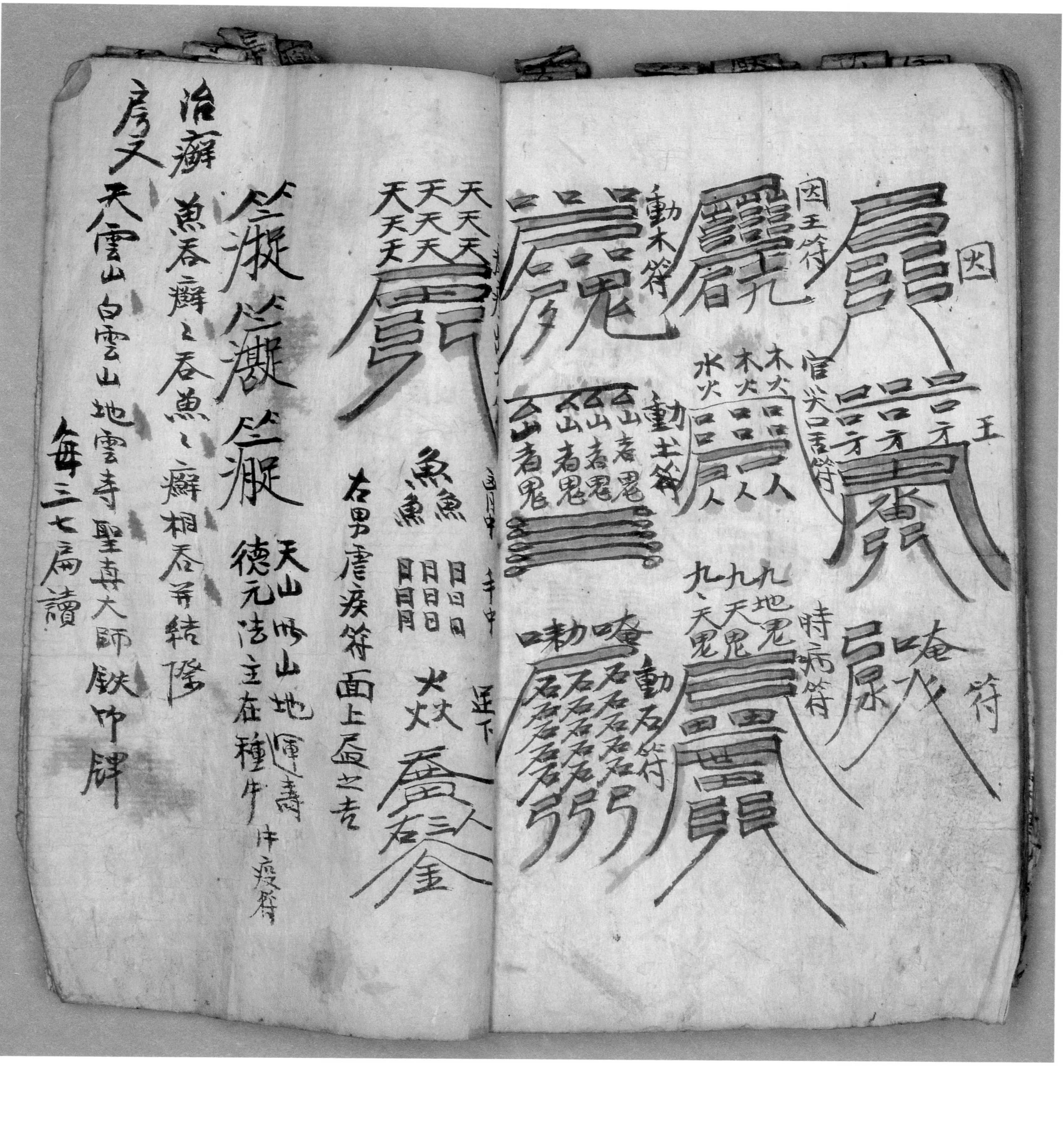

囚王符　官災口舌符　動木符　動土符　時病符

木火□□　動石符
木火山
水火

地鬼　九天鬼　動石符
天鬼　九天鬼

天天天
天天天

右男唐疾符面上孟之吉

魚魚　　曰曰曰
魚魚　　曰曰曰

手中　廷下

犬炎　唐疫符

竺凝竺凝　竺凝

天山哪山地運壽
德元法主在種牛

治癖　魚吞癖之吞魚之癖相吞等結陰

彦文　天人雲山白雲山地雲寺聖壽大師鐵巾牌

每三七扁讀

Amulets (pujŏk) in an old shamanist manual

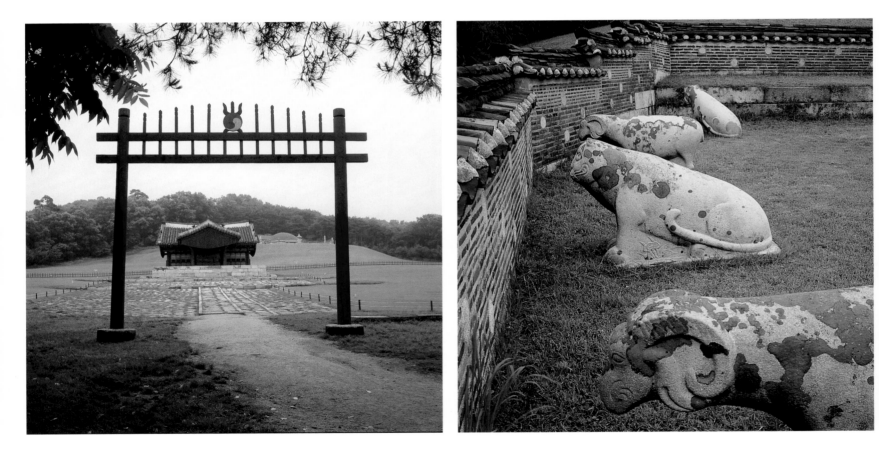

Hongsalmun, *a typical Korean red gateway*
with bars on top, in front of the Kŏn-nŭng,
the tomb of King Chŏngjo (ruled 1776-1800),
in Hwasan, Hwasŏng-gun, Kyŏnggi-do.

Animal statues at the same tomb

A *Seven Star* (Ch'ilsŏng) *Shrine. The icons in the interior*
reveal a combination of Buddhism
and shamanism. The exterior door leading into
the rocky shrine has the Big Dipper constellation
designed with silver stars

In Magok-sa we find influences of Lamaism
(introduced during the period
of Mongol domination, 1231-1356).
Here we see figures in part of a karma-maṇḍala;
in Lamaism the pig's heads symbolize
human stupidity (a maṇḍala *is a symbolic diagram)*

The bell tower of T'ongdosa.
The four instruments used
in Buddhist ceremonies are: the temple bell,
the wooden fish, the cloud-shaped metal unp'an
and the drum. These four instruments symbolize
the transmission of the 'sound of the Buddha'

Magok-sa. The wooden fish is a percussion instru-
ment made from a log which has been hollowed out
from the bottom and carved in the shape of a fish.
As a fish never closes its eyes, it is exemplary
for those who lead a monastic life

The nunnery of Ŭnmun-sa, not far from Taegu.
The drum calls for salvation from purgatory
or the World of Beasts

Hwaŏm-sa on Chi[r]i-san. A monk strikes
the large temple bell during
the morning worship ceremony

Gilt bronze Bhaiṣajyaguru (national treasure no. 337)
in Changgok-sa. The temple is protected at the rear
by a hill

Religion and philosophy

It is no easy task to handle the religions of Korea in a relatively brief chapter. We shall inevitably have to limit ourselves in certain ways, which will be dictated primarily by our pictorial material.

In our remarks on the history of Korea we noted that Buddhism was the state religion for one millennium and that Neo-Confucianism became the state philosophy during the Chosŏn dynasty and remained so for five hundred years. Buddhism is both a philosophy and a religion; Confucianism is a moral philosophy that developed religious traits, hence the title of this chapter.

Taoism was officially introduced to Korea twice, the first time in Koguryŏ in the first half of the seventh century, the second time in Koryŏ in 1107. The idea behind recognizing Taoism as a religion was based on the – Chinese – view that 'the three doctrines (Buddhism, Confucianism and Taoism) are like the feet of a tripod and it is impossible that one should be lacking.' These endeavors notwithstanding, Taoism was never able to gain equal standing with the other two religions in Korea. Only in shamanism and in folk religion do we find quite a number of influences from vulgar Taoism.

The basis of geomantic theories is the knowledge of the proper distribution of the two cosmic forces, *ŭm* and *yang* (Chin. *yin* and *yang*). The basic meanings of the characters for *ŭm* and *yang* are the northern and southern sides of a mountain, i.e., the shady side and the sunny side. *Ŭm* is cold, moist, dark, tranquil, female, etc.; *yang* is hot, dry, bright, active, male, etc. The two forces are complementary and together they maintain the cosmic harmony. The quantity of *ŭm* and *yang*, or the interaction between them, is not constant. Each of the two powers regularly increases and decreases again.

The activity of *ŭm* and *yang* in the earth is called *sallyŏng*, 'mountain spirit, mountain energy'; it emanates as a sort of aura. When selecting the proper location for a palace, a private residence, a grave, etc., the influence of this aura must be taken into consideration. Because the quantitative and qualitative existence of *sallyŏng* is determined by the atmospheric and tellurian influences within a given landscape, geomancy is called *p'ungsu* (Chin. *fengshui*), 'wind and water.' Numerology and the doctrine of the five elements (wood, fire, earth, metal and water) also play a role in geomancy.

We reported rather extensively on the introduction of Christianity and the persecution of Christians associated therewith in the chapter on history (Chosŏn dynasty, second period). A few additional remarks are in order here. Yi Sŭnghun, who was baptized in Peking at the end of the eighteenth century, was not the first Korean Christian. During the Japanese invasion in 1592, the Portuguese missionary Gregorio de Cespedes accompanied the Christian general, Konishi Yukinaga (d. 1600), and when he returned to Japan (1595) he took a Korean boy with him. The boy, who was about 13 years old at the time, was christened Vincent and brought up by the Jesuits. He was ordained a priest in 1626. In the same year he was put to death in Nagasaki, the first Korean martyr. The world traveler Francesco Carletti, who was in Japan in 1597–1598, reports that he bought five Korean slaves there and had them baptized. The above mentioned Konishi took a Korean girl along and raised her in his family. She was baptized and served the first Tokugawa shogun, Ieyasu (1542–1616), as a court lady in the palaces of Fushimi and Sunpu (= Shizuoka). In 1612 she was banned to Ōshima (an island east of Izu) for being a Christian. Her name was Julia Otā (or Vota).

After the country had been opened to trade with the Western powers, Protestant (mostly American) missionaries of various confessions began their activities. Worthy of mention are their accomplishments in the field of education. In June 1886 the Methodist missionary Mary F. Scranton founded the first girls' school, which was named by the Korean queen Ihwa Haktang, 'Pear Blossom Academy.' This educational institution (Ewha University/Ihwa Taehakkyo), with more than 9000 students, is the largest women's university in the world. In March 1915 the Presbyterian missionary Horace G. Underwood founded Chosen Christian College (Korean name: Yŏnhŭi Taehak); in 1957 it was combined with Severance Union Medical College and renamed Yonsei (Yŏnse) University. Ewha and Yonsei are among the best universities in the country.

The growth of Christianity in Korea, especially after the Second World War, is astonishing. In 1989 there were 6,489,000 Protestant Christians in South Korea and 1,865,000 Catholics, which means that it had become the most highly Christianized country in the Far East, after the Philippines.

Sosu sŏwŏn in Sunhŭng County, Kyŏngsang Pukto.
This private Confucian school is dedicated
to the memory of the famous scholar An Hyang
(1243-1306).

The burial site has to be chosen according
to geomantic principles. Selecting an auspicious burial site
for one's parents is a filial duty

Am, 'hermitage', near Pŏpchu-sa.
As with all temples, this building also faces the south

Shamanism

In the Three Kingdoms period shamanism already played an important role. The kings of Koguryŏ and Paekche consulted shamanesses about the fate of their countries and had their diseases cured by them. The early rulers of Silla were themselves shamans.

In the Koryŏ and Chosŏn periods shamans and shamanesses are mentioned as performing at official ceremonies and important palace celebrations. Nonetheless, they belonged to the lowest class of society. In many cases their services were evidently indispensable. People in modern Korea, particularly the intelligentsia and Christians, tend to look down on shamans. Public authorities often view their 'primitive' activities as a disgrace for a civilized nation.

Be that as it may, there still are many shamans. More than two thirds of them are women, who are generally referred to as *mudang*. The male shaman is usually called a *paksu*. The Korean shamans do not travel to heaven or hell, but they are possessed by gods or spirits when in trance or ecstasy. They perform when people request protection or favors from gods and spirits: when dedicating new buildings, at ship launchings, to cure disease or to dispatch the soul of a deceased person to the other world.

For the most part the profession of shaman is hereditary. In the case of the *mudang*, it is passed down from mother to daughter or daughter-in-law. In addition, there are persons who are chosen by the spirits, so to speak. This category includes blind and mentally unstable shamans (the blind can perceive things that are hidden from other people). Third, there are people who choose this profession for economic reasons, for it can be quite profitable!

The *mudang* and *paksu* of the first category have their own ancestors, who enjoy particular veneration in their pantheon.

The host of gods, spirits and demons that exert influences on human life is summed up by the Sino-Korean term *kwisin*. We can classify them as follows:

1 celestial deities and spirits (e.g., Hananim, the Korean ruler of Heaven; Okhwang Sangje, the supreme ruler in Chinese Taoism; the Buddhas and Bodhisattvas; the deities of the celestial bodies);
2 earthly deities and spirits, among whom we find deified Chinese and Korean heroes and other great personages;

3 the tutelary spirits of the house (including the House Lord, the Foundation God, the Kitchen God and the Toilet Maiden);
4 earth spirits that preside over a certain area and its commercial products (this group includes mountain spirits, dragon kings and the tutelary deities of certain areas, cf. below). Outside of this classification we have goblins, will-o'-the-wisps, animals with supernatural powers and sacred plants.

In the house of a hereditary shaman family one almost always finds a room that is called a *sindang*, 'spirit hall.' In this shrine an altar, images of Buddhas, Bodhisattvas and spirits and such equipment as clothing, mirrors, drums, bells, spears and swords are stored. There are also shrines whose use is shared by several *mudang* or *paksu*, and permanent or temporary natural shrines (places in the open in which spirits live or sojourn at certain times). Of course at times people order a *mudang* to their houses.

During the ceremonies of exorcism, *kut*, the *mudang* dances, sings, recites prayers and incantations and transmits the 'spirits' words' (a *mudang* can, e.g., speak with the voice of a deceased person). A *kut* consists of several acts (*kŏri*) – usually twelve – and can take a whole day.

Shaman dancers painted on the ceiling of Pŏm'ŏ-sa.
Heavenly musicians function to placate
the shamanist Roofbeam Spirit with their dances,
to maintain the integrity of the structure

During the kut, *the* mudang *(sorceress)*
regularly changes costume. Ecstatic dances
form an essential part of the ceremony

*Along the road are often found colored rags
hanging as offerings in front of small altars*

Outdoor dance pageant in traditional style

A table with sacrificial offerings
at a shamanist ceremony of exorcism

Shamanistic ritual in conjunction
with a firm's acquisition of a new safe.
Offerings are made to the gods for enhanced prosperity

Some Tutelary Deities

The menhirs of prehistoric times served to demarcate a certain area; at the same time they probably were supposed to protect the area and its inhabitants from evil spirits that might bring harm or disease.

The kingdom of Silla had its own tutelary godesses who lived at its borders. Dragons and mountain and earth spirits could appear as tutelary deities or spirits. The Korean house has many tutelary spirits, among whom Chesŏk or Sejon watches over the life and death of all members of the family.

We should like to first turn our attention to three objects that particularly strike one's eye during a trip around the country: the *sŏnang* (sacred trees or stone heaps), the *changsŭng* (wooden spirit posts) and the *sottae* (bird poles).

The Polish visitor to Korea, W. Sieroszewski, in his still invaluable book *Korea* (1904, p. 30–31, cf. bibliography) reported the following:

'Korea's streets are abundantly covered with altars, divine images and sacred trees. Most frequently one encounters the *sŏuhoan-dang* (= *sŏnghwang-dan*) – the altars of the holy ruler. These are usually low heaps of rocks casually piled up under an old tree or in a small grove. Usually there is no idol, not even a picture. Bits of paper, colored rags, ribbons, little bags with rice, torn hats and worn-out shoes hang as offerings left by pious travelers on the branches of the trees. Occasionally there stand beside them small, wretched shrines, erected in honor of the animals and birds that destroy harmful insects...

'Often at the entrance to a village or when leaving it I saw posts, as tall as a man or more; the ends were carved, represented human faces painted red, white or black and were often even adorned with Korean hats.

'My Tonsa (= *t'ongsa*, interpreter), who was very reluctant to give any explanations of things related to religion, incessantly asserted that these were signposts... Only after I pointed out several times that according to his own statements 'signposts' were shorter, had an inscription and were erected at a distance of at least 10 li (5 verst) – which was not true in this case – he admitted that they were *ghosts*. But he did not wish to confide any more particulars. He also refused to give an explanation of the around 10–15 feet high bird poles, whose tips were decorated with wooden images of birds and with straw ropes hang-

Little stone towers and other elements of shamanism can be found all over in Korea. Note the small altar under the tree

ing from the tails of the birds. Usually such poles were set up in pairs at the entrance to a village.'

In most of the other old travel accounts only *changsŭng* are mentioned, they being the most striking, and they are referred to as idols, signposts or milestones.

The name *sŏnghwang* (also *sŏngwang* or *sŏnang*) is Chinese in origin: *ch'eng-huang*; the concept is undoubtedly Korean. Ch'eng-huang[-yeh] is in China the god of the city walls and moats; in Korea *sŏnang* were originally the tutelary spirits of the boundaries of a certain area and later developed into the tutelary spirits of the area within these boundaries. They have their own shrines and altars: *sŏnang-dang*.

Passers-by often hang scraps of paper on which they have written their wishes, remnants of clothing, old straw sandals, etc. as votive offerings on the twigs of sacred trees (*sŏnang-namu*); now and then they throw a new stone on the pile of rocks as a mark of respect. In Mongolia similar stone heaps are found, which serve as the residence and gathering place of the local tutelary deities and spirits. There they are called *obo*.

Changsŭng are mentioned for the first time in history under the name *changsaeng p'yoju*, 'pillars of long life.' In the fourth decade of the tenth century these pillars were used as boundary posts to mark off the area belonging to a temple. In the fifteenth century they were also used as milestones and in the next century as 'prohibition poles' on which, e.g., 'no fishing' was written (at Buddhist temples).

Evidently *changsŭng* is a garbled form of *changsaeng*. One usually finds these posts made of pine wood at the entrance to villages, along the way up to Buddhist temples and at the side of the road. Occasionally several are found in a group tied together with a sacred straw rope (*kŭmjul* or *inchul*) to ward off evil influences. Where a pair of *changsŭng* is found, on the upper part of the male figure *ch'ŏnha taejanggun* (supreme commander of the world) is usually written or carved, on the lower part of the female figure, *chiha yŏjanggun* (woman commander of the underground).

With their repulsive appearance, their main task as tutelary deities is to ward off harm and evil spirits; they also have the magic power to cure disease. They additionally used to be used as signposts or milestones; the distance to the next village was then given in *li* (1 *li* = 536 m).

On Cheju-do the *tol-mirŭk*, 'stone Maitreyas' have

a comparable function to that of the *changsŭng* on the mainland (cf. Cheju-do in the chapter on geography, nature and landscape).

Posts or poles with an aquatic bird (grebe?) roughly carved of wood sitting on top of them are called *susaltae*, *susalmagi* or *sottae*. Now and then they are encountered with the *changsŭng*. The first two names mean 'posts of water killing'; these poles therefore served to placate the evil influences of the water (floods and the like). Examining them in more detail, we discover that these posts also served to demarcate a certain area and to protect its inhabitants. In this context the term *sottae* becomes interesting. Among the Han tribes, especially the Mahan, in the first century A.D., there were so-called *sodo* or *sottae*, sacred places under the custody of a priest. On a *sodo* there were an altar and some tall trees, in which bells and drums were hung. This sacred place was a kind of asylum, where robbers and other criminals took refuge. Presumably the term *sottae* was transferred from the place to the poles, probably because they came to be identified with the trees standing there.

The last tutelary deity we should briefly mention is the *haet'ae*, an animal usually sculpted of stone that looks like a cross between a lion and a dog. On its head it almost always has a short horn. It comes from China, where it is called *hsieh-ch'ih* or *hsieh-chai* and has the power to distinguish between good and evil. It destroys evil persons. In Korea the *haet'ae* is capable of eating fire. One finds *haet'ae* in pairs in front of the main gates of palaces, in front of Buddhist temples, graves and bridges, to protect them from fire.

Male spirit posts (changsŭng).
To the left of the middle one a sottae *is standing*

Female spirit posts (changsŭng)
accompanied by a sottae

142

Nature worship at a grotto on Kyeryong-san

Small altar in a rock cave

The Mountain Spirit

In a mountainous country like Korea the Mountain Spirit (*sansin*; also *sallyŏng taesin*, 'great spirit of mountain energy') is particularly important and deserves a section of its own.

It belongs to the category of earth spirits and can also appear as the tutelary deity of the village at the foot of the mountain over which it presides. People pray to it for success when gathering berries, mushrooms and herbs. It is particularly revered by ginseng hunters, who spend weeks on end in the forest during the summer.

In the shrines to the mountain spirit (*sansindang*), which often stand at the entrance to forests, the mountain spirit is represented as a venerable old man accompanied by or riding a tiger, which is considered his vassal or courier. There can be little doubt that the tiger – itself an animal with supernatural powers – is the personification of the mountain spirit and that the old man was added later. In the course of time the mountain spirit has acquired a wife, Young Lady Mountain Spirit (*sansin agassi*) or Old Lady Mountain Spirit (*sansin manura*). On occasion women pray to the Mountain Spirit for children (because of confusion between the terms *sansin* and *samsin*, the birth spirit?).

Buddhism

The Buddhism that we encounter in China, Korea and Japan is primarily Mahāyāna, the 'Greater Vehicle,' which emerged in India shortly before the birth of Christ. Characteristic of Mahāyāna is the notion that the world of material phenomena (i.e., not of non-existing phenomena, but of relatively existing phenomena) and Nirvāṇa, 'extinction,' are different manifestations of the Absolute that is the basis of the Universe. This Absolute is the eternal and universal Buddha nature, with which one can identify oneself by means of transcendental insight (γνωσις, *prajñā*). Referring to the Buddha nature, certain Mahāyāna scriptures proclaim that all living beings possess the seeds of Buddhahood equally and are therefore capable of realizing Buddhahood. Illusion prevents these seeds from taking effect, however. If Illusion is destroyed, the seeds come into their own and Enlightenment is attained.

This cardinal theme is elaborated differently by the various Mahāyāna sects. In the mystic Chin'ŏn sect, e.g., the 'womb world' of phenomena (so called because the phenomena emerge from it as from a womb) and the 'diamond world,' i.e., the world of ideas/the world of the Absolute are contrasted. For him who attains the highest insight there is no difference between the two worlds. This highest insight is identical with Enlightenment. The Chin'ŏn doctrine was introduced from China in 665 by the Silla monk Hyet'ong (*chin'ŏn* = true word, i.e., mystic formulas, Sanskrit: *mantra*).

In Buddhism the 'self' is a complex of five *skandhas* (accumulations or aggregates, Sino-Korean *on*), which are at no moment identical, but are continuously subject to change. These *skandhas* (1 shape/matter = body, 2 feelings, 3 discernments, 4 volitional factors, 5 consciousness) could be called the physical and psychic components or life elements of the human pseudopersonality. All five *skandhas* (only one of which refers to matter, the others to mental functions) are equivalent and coordinated, but – as we said – they are *per se* inconstant.

In the world of phenomena the relentless law of causality prevails: *karman* (act, work, consequence > fate [usually referred to in the West since the spread of theosophy and the popularization of Buddhism as *karma*]). After the human body has ceased to func-

Pongjŏng-sa near Andong, Kyŏngsang Pukto.
Shrine to Sansin, the Mountain Spirit.
Visitors to Buddhist temples often pay their respects
to Sansin as well

Painted portal at Pong'ŭn-sa,
'Receiving Grace Temple,' in Kwangju County,
Kyŏnggi-do. Dates originally from 794

Small path leading to the Pŏm'ŏ-sa

The Ch'ŏn'wang-mun,
'The Gate of the Four Heavenly Guardians',
at Sŏn'un-sa, Koch'ang County, Chŏlla Pukto.
In the background, the main hall of the temple

High above the sea in Yangyang County, Kangwŏn-do,
lies Naksan-sa. The temple was founded in 671 bij Ŭisang
(625-702)

Temple lantern in Porim-sa, Changhŭng County, Chŏlla Namdo. This temple originated as a simple straw hut built by the Sŏn priest Pojo in 860

tion, i.e., after death, the *skandhas* – because of their inherent yearning for continuity – have the power to take on a new form, to be reincarnated. The new personality that has then emerged is predetermined by the *karman* of the previous life – by a *karman* that is determined not only by every physical action but also by each and every word and thought. We are not speaking here of an eternal, immutable soul (and thus not of a 'transmigration of souls'), but in a certain sense one could speak of immortality. In this perpetual reincarnation process man is a prisoner of suffering – a suffering that is caused by desire. Relief from suffering is only possible by release from desire, i.e., by destroying the self-seeking zest for life: the extinction of the 'self,' the complete cessation of phenomenal existence. This release can be achieved through the above mentioned transcendental insight and corresponds to attaining Nirvāṇa, from which there is no return to new reincarnations.

There are two paths by which one can break through the cycle of rebirth. One path is the doctrine of the Pure Land, according to which one can, by living a virtuous life and trusting in the mercy of Amitābha Buddha, be reborn in his Paradise. There one can mature into Nirvāṇa. The Pure Land is Sukhāvatī (Sino-Korean Chŏngt'o), the Western Paradise, reigned over by Amitābha, 'whose light is boundless' (Sino-Korean Amit'a). The more often the believer repeats the prayer formula, *Nam[m]u Amit'a-bul*, 'homage to Amitābha Buddha,' the greater is the effect. In popular Buddhism Paradise contrasts with the netherworld, which is divided into several sections (hells). Yama-rāja (Sino-Korean Yŏmma Wang) is the king and judge. He passes judgment on the misdeeds of the deceased and delivers them up to the devils for punishment. Because the netherworld, like Paradise, is a transitional state, a term such as purgatory might be more appropriate.

The Pure Land School was introduced to Silla by Wŏnhyo (617–686), whose great merit was to have popularized Buddhism. On the other hand, he also wrote a number of philosophical treatises. He can also be considered the founder of the typically Korean *t'ong-bulgyo*, 'universal Buddhism,' i.e., an attempt to combine all trends and schools in one great whole – a kind of Buddhist ecumenism.

The second path by which one can break through the reincarnation process is that of Sŏn, better known in the West under its Sino-Japanese name, Zen. Sŏn is an abbreviation of *sŏnna* (Sino-Japanese *zenna*, Chinese *ch'anna*), a rendition of the Sanskrit *dhyāna*, 'absorption, meditation.' The essence of Sŏn is to achieve Enlightenment by one's own power, and the path that one should follow is prescribed in four rules:

1 the nonrecognition of canonical scriptures,
2 a special tradition outside the traditional teachings (transmission from mind to mind),
3 direct reference to the human heart (mind),
4 the attainment of Buddhahood through insight into one's own nature.

The last two rules culminate in sudden enlightenment. In this life (here and now) one can realize Nirvāṇa through a sudden insight into the Absolute achieved in a state of mental void. In other words: comprehending one's own Buddha nature by breaking through conscious, logical thought.

This enlightenment, through which a *unio mystica* with the Buddha nature is achieved, does not imply a retiring-from-the-world. On the contrary, Sŏn encourages participation in the life of this world – a participation that should be distinguished from an egocentric type of involvement, which entails conflicts and spiritual breakdowns.

Contemplation exercises known as *sŏn (dhyāna)* are cultivated in all Buddhist sects. Sŏn as a special method of approaching the teachings of Buddha was introduced to Korea in the eighth century. It evidently appealed strongly to the Koreans. After its introduction and spread in Silla two types of Buddhism were distinguished: that of the Five Schools (represented by five sects) and that of the Nine Mountains, i.e., the nine Sŏn temples, which represented the different branches of Sŏn in the Unified Silla state. Around 1100, i.e., in the Koryŏ period, the Sŏn branches of the Nine Mountains were usually combined under the name Chogye-jong, 'Chogye Sect.' The most important representative and reformer of the Chogye Sect was Chinul (1158–1210), who 'favored a gradual cultivation of the mind toward sudden enlightenment' (i.e., he did not absolutely reject knowledge of the canonical scriptures).

In the chapter on History we saw that Buddhism was suppressed during the Chosŏn period and Neo-Confucianism was proclaimed state doctrine. In 1424 all Buddhist sects were combined in the Sŏnjong

(Contemplative School) and the Kyojong (Textual School). In modern Korea we find nineteen Buddhist sects, of which the Chogye-jong, that is the Sŏn sect, is the largest. According to official statistics there were 8,060,000 Buddhists in Korea in 1989.

The Buddha (Sino-Korean Puch'ŏ, Pult'a, Pul), the 'Illumined One,' of our era (*kalpa*) was born as Siddharta Gautama in 563 B.C. in a forest near the village of Lumbinī (not far from the city of Kapilavastu) and entered Nirvāṇa in 483 B.C. Buddha's birthday is celebrated in Korea each year on the eighth of April. Because Siddharta belonged to the noble Śākya clan, he is often referred to as Śākyamuni (*muni* = sage, ascetic). At the age of sixteen he was married and thirteen years later he had a son named Rāhula. Soon thereafter he grew weary of life as a member of the Indian noble caste and became a mendicant monk. He studied under several teachers, cultivated an ascetic life and wandered around. Not until 528 B.C., at the age of 35, did he attain Enlightenment (*bodhi*, perfect wisdom).

Buddha's teachings were written down after his death in *sūtras*, prose texts, which usually take the form of sermons or discourses (*sūtras*, Sino-Korean *kyŏng*, = thread > holy cord). For the most part they are found in the second division (*sūtra-piṭaka*) of the Buddhist canon, the *Tripiṭaka*. The *Tripiṭaka*, the 'Three Baskets' (Sino-Korean *Samjang* or *Taejang-gyŏng*) is composed of three compartments: the basket of disciplines (for monastic life), the basket of teachings and the basket of metaphysics. The individual texts are known as *sūtras* and *śāstras* (treatises, Sino-Korean *non*, *-ron*).

As the Buddha of our era, Śākyamuni of course had many predecessors in earlier ages and he will have many successors in future *kalpas*. Moreover – according to the Mahāyāna view – all other creatures of a given era can attain Buddhahood. From this it follows that there are innumerable Buddhas.

A Buddha has three bodies (*trikāya*, Sino-Korean *samsin*), i.e., manifestations or aspects:

1 the body of the law (*dharmakāya*), which is identical with the Absolute;
2 the body of bliss (*saṃbhogakāya*), which appears to the believer in its supernatural splendor;
3 the body of transmutation (*nirmāṇakāya*), i.e., Buddha as a human being.

Applied to the historical Buddha, Śākyamuni (Korean Sŏkka[moni]) is his body of transmutation; Amitāyus, 'whose life span is boundless,' is his body of bliss; and Amitābha, 'whose light is boundless,' his body of the law. As was to be expected, in East Asia the two latter aspects became confused. Amitābha and Amitāyus are both called Amit'a in Korea. When people speak of Amit'a, they generally mean the Buddha of the Western Paradise (the Pure Land), in other words, Amitāyus. Amit'a is, however, almost always interpreted as being identical with Amitābha.

Mahāvairocana Tathāgata, the 'Great Sun Buddha' (Sino-Korean Tae'il Yŏrae) or Vairocana (Korean Pirojana) is the supreme or primordial Buddha (*tathāgata*, 'he who has thus arrived, the Perfect One,' Sino-Korean *yŏrae*, is an honorary title for a Buddha). In the esoteric sects he is revered as the body of the Law (the absolute reality), from which all other Buddhas, all living beings and everything that exists arose.

Bhaiṣajyaguru, the 'teacher of medicine' (Sino-Korean Yaksa Yŏrae), reigns in the Eastern Paradise. He is revered above all as the Buddha who heals the sick and is therefore very popular.

In addition to these Buddhas, Mahāyāna knows Bodhisattvas, 'beings, whose nature is perfect wisdom' (Sino-Korean Posal). They are 'aspirants to Buddhahood,' beings who postpone their own entrance into Nirvāṇa and out of compassion strive to redeem others. One could therefore consider a Bodhisattva a kind of Buddhist Savior.

The most important Bodhisattva is Maitreya (Sino-Korean Mirŭk), the Buddha of the next era, the future Buddha, who is preparing himself for his duties in the Tuṣita Heaven. He is erroneously referred to as Mirŭk Pul, the 'Buddha Maitreya,' instead of Mirŭk Posal.

Avalokiteśvara (Sino-Korean Kwan[se]ŭm), 'Lord, who looks down from above,' is the transformation of the redeeming mercy of Amitābha. Tibet's Dalai Lāma is an incarnation of this Bodhisattva. Probably because he is portrayed as the ideal of beauty, Avalokiteśvara changed in China from a male to a female Bodhisattva. His name in East Asia (in China, Kuan-[shih-]yin, in Japan, Kan[ze]on > Kannon, in Korea, cf. above) means 'he who looks down at (listens to) the sounds (i.e., prayers) of the world' and stems from an incorrect analysis and thus false translation of his Sanskrit name. The female Kwanseŭm (who

Ssanggye-sa, Hadong County, Kyŏngsang Namdo, was founded by Priest Sambŏp in 723 during the Silla period.
Entrance to a small hermitage

In the Myŏngbu-jŏn, the Hall of Judgment, in Buddhist temples stand terrifying guardians and ten wise judges. They also represent some pre-Buddhist conceptions.
Chŏndŭng-sa, Kanghwa-do

150

The 'thousand Buddhas' of the past,
present and future under a very nicely decorated ceiling.
In Ŭnmun-sa, a nunnery not far from Taegu

Picturesque section of a roof in Tonghak-sa

*Main hall of Magok-sa in Kongju County,
Ch'ungch'ŏng Namdo*

*Buddhist paintings on the outside wall
of a temple*

*Praying nun rising from prostrated position,
at Ŭnmun-sa*

152

can, though very rarely, appear in Korea in the guise of a male) is a Goddess of Mercy, so to speak, a helper in time of need, to whom one can pray for children, for instance.

Kṣitigarbha, 'whose womb is the earth' (Sino-Korean Chijang), saves sinners, especially children, from the netherworld.

In the iconography Samantabhadra, 'he who is entirely good' (Sino-Korean Pohyŏn), and Mañjuśrī, 'he whose beauty is charming' (Sino-Korean Munsu), are the attendants of the historical Buddha. Pohyŏn, at Buddha's right side (riding a white elephant), symbolizes his supreme kindness, Munsu, on his left (riding a lion), his omniscience.

Important in the iconography are the gestures of the hands and fingers, *mudrās* (Sino-Korean *in* or *ingye*), of the Buddhas or Bodhisattvas. We shall mention only one example: Sŏkkamoni's right hand often touches the earth (calls it to witness) while the left hand lies on his lap, its palm turned upward (gesture of meditation).

Apart from the Buddhas and Bodhisattvas Korean Buddhism knows other saints, which originated in India, the Arhats and Devas. The Arhats (Sino-Korean Nahan) are borrowed from Hīnayāna, the 'Lesser Vehicle,' i.e., the older form of Buddhism. They attain Nirvāṇa for themselves through their own striving. As a title Arhat is conferred on the sixteen most important disciples of the historical Buddha. In art the Arhats are usually depicted in groups of 10, 16, 18 or 500.

Devas are gods and demons that are borrowed from the Indian non-Buddhist pantheon. Among them we find the Four Heavenly Kings (Sino-Korean Sach'ŏnwang), the guardians of the world, who appear in Korea as temple guardians and drive away demons.

One enters the grounds of a Buddhist temple from the south through one or several gates (*mun*). The most important building is the main hall (Tae'ungjŏn), which contains the statue of the particular Buddha who is worshipped in this temple (Tae'ung, 'great hero,' is one of the honorary titles for a Buddha). Other buildings are the bell tower, possibly some subsidiary temples (e.g., for worshipping Kwanseŭm), the longish buildings housing the cells for the monks, pagodas and pagoda-like stone lanterns. In the larger buildings the eaves bracketing and the friezes are almost always worthy of notice.

The bell tower (*chonggak* or *chongnu*) is an open, pavilion-like building. The bronze bell (*chong*) is often decorated with leaf and tendril motifs, animal figures (dragon, serpent), floating angels playing musical instruments, sometimes with inscriptions in relief. The bell does not have a clapper and is therefore not 'rung,' but hit from outside with a wooden beam that hangs on ropes or chains for this purpose.

The pagoda (*t'ap*) comes from the Indian *stūpa*, originally meaning a hill in which an urn containing the remains of an outstanding personality was kept. Later the term meant a tower-like structure for storing relics. In Korea the four, six and eight-sided (rarely round) pagodas, which can have 3, 5, 7, 9, 10, or 13 stories, hold the mortal remains or other relics of holy persons, pictures of saints and sacred scriptures. In many cases they can be thought of as votive monuments.

A remarkable thing is that within the temple grounds there is usually a shamanist shrine to the Mountain Spirit (*sansin-dang*). At remote temples in the mountains one can also find a pavilion for the Seven Star Spirit (*ch'ilsŏng-gak*) – a further concession to popular beliefs.

Tonghak-sa on the eastern slope of Kyeryong-san, Ch'ungch'ŏng Namdo

Doors painted with flower and leaf motifs

*Three thousand porcelain images
surrounding the gilt bronze Buddha
enshrined on the altar. This is the work
of Monk Sŏngp'a from a hermitage near T'ongdo-sa*

Mysterious Buddhist statues
in the 'Valley of Thousand Buddhas and Thousand Pagodas'.
Unju-sa, Hwasun County in Chŏlla Namdo

Rock cut Buddhist image. This rare relief of Buddha
seated on a chair is a designated national treasure.
Pŏpchu-sa

Buddhist 'Goddess of Mercy' at Naksan-sa

Sŏkkamoni with his right hand held
in the vitarka-mudrā, *the gesture of bearing witness.*
In Pulguk-sa, the 'Buddhaland Temple'

A very modern statue
of the 'Goddess of Mercy' at Pŏpchu-sa

Chikchi-sa. Seated Buddha
in front of a painting of Bhaiṣajyaguru

A modern Buddhist temple in Seoul

Bell tower of a modern temple *Pŏm'ŏ-sa. Monks' dormitory*

*Worshipping the primordial Buddha
(Mahāvairocana) in Haein-sa*

*The monks begin their prayers before dawn.
T'ongdo-sa*

Early morning ceremony at Ŭnmun-sa

*Monks returning to their study rooms
after the late evening ceremony. Haein-sa*

High in the mountains we find a pavilion for meditation

Stūpa *of the Sŏn priest Chinul (1158-1210),*
Songgwang-sa in Sŭngju County, Chŏlla Namdo

Koun-sa. Meditating monk.
Sŏn attempts to transcend language
and empty the mind to achieve Enlightenment

Funeral ceremony in Changgok-sa.
The family of the deceased are wearing
hemp mourning clothes

Monk at prayer

Offering of food and wine. The Koreans believe that
the souls of the deceased continue to live with them

Memorial tablets for deceased persons

Confucianism

Confucianism is a moral philosophy. Its name is derived from that of the Chinese philosopher K'ung Fu-tze, Master K'ung (551–479 B.C.), latinized by the Jesuit missionaries in China as Confucius. In Korea he is referred to as Kongja, Master Kong.

Confucius was born as K'ung Ch'iu to a down-at-the-heels noble family in the feudal state of Lu (in the present-day province of Shantung). He studied the history, rites (ceremonials) and music of antiquity and was particularly fascinated by the political and social system of the Western Chou dynasty (eleventh to eighth century B.C.), which he idealized and strove to revive. He held several offices in Lu, but when he was 55, he began a period of wandering that was to last for thirteen years. Together with a number of students he traveled from the court of one prince to another in the feudal China of the period and proclaimed his philosophical and political ideas, which were not always received with appreciation. At the age of 68 (in 484 B.C.) he returned from his wanderings to Lu, where he continued to serve as a philosopher and teacher.

Having developed in a feudal age, Confucianism is fundamentally a doctrine of inequality. Within the extremes of the highest and lowest, each and every member of society has his superiors and his subordinates. Whereas the subordinates owe their superiors obedience and respect, superiors should treat their subordinates with responsibility and benevolence.

The five basic relationships between people are called *wu-lun* (Sino-Korean *oryun*). They are the relationships between ruler and civil servant (or subject), father and son, man and wife, older brother and younger brother, friend and friend. The paramount obligation in the first relationship is loyalty (*chung*, Sino-Korean *ch'ung*), in the second filial piety (*hsiao*, Sino-Korean *hyo*).

The above mentioned relationships between persons in society and within the family are supposed to be based on the five cardinal virtues, *wu-ch'ang* (*osang*): *jen* (*in*), 'benevolence or human-heartedness'; *i* (*ŭi*), 'righteousness'; *li* (*ye*) 'etiquette'; *chih* (*chi*), 'wisdom'; *hsin* (*sin*), 'trust' (the expressions in parentheses are the Sino-Korean equivalents of the Chinese terms).

Benevolence or human-heartedness is not Chris-

tian charity, but 'not doing to others what you do not like yourself' (*Lun-yü* XII, 2). The *Lun-yü* (*Analects of Confucius*), which we have just quoted and will quote frequently in the following, contains the conversations and sayings of Confucius, which were probably not collected until the beginning of the fourth century A.D.

Righteousness is interpreted as *suum cuique* (to each his own) or 'knowledge of the correct social distinctions.'

Etiquette is correct behavior, which guarantees proper order in society.

Wisdom does not refer to scientific knowledge. It should be comprehended as *sagesse* not *intellectualité*. Confucian literati cultivated philosophy not for the sake of science; their goal was primarily to develop man's inherent 'natural' goodness.

The Chinese character that stands for the term 'trust' is composed of the two elements 'man' and 'word': 'a man and his word.' Further explanation would be superfluous.

It is noteworthy that many old Chinese terms took on a new meaning in Confucianism. *Li*, e.g., originally referred to religious rites, in particular to the external rites for the dead and for the ancestors. Confucius transformed the meaning of the term to an internal mental attitude toward life, to a system of personal ethics combined with correct external behavior vis-à-vis one's fellow man.

The term *tao* ('way' > the course of things in nature, that which constitutes all that happens) lost its metaphysical content in Confucius' hands, for the most part, and is used primarily in an ethical sense. It is related particularly to the ideal social order: 'The Master did not discuss the *tao* of Heaven' (*Lun-yü* V, 12).

Te (the magic power of an ideal ruler) no longer has the old Chinese sense of *virtus*, but that of 'virtue, moral superiority.' A last example of 'bourgeoisification' in Confucian terminology is *chün-tze*, originally a term of rank meaning ruler's son. Confucius no longer uses the two-syllable term – usually translated as 'gentleman' – in the sense of 'aristocrat,' but as 'virtuous ideal person.' This transition from hereditary nobility to spiritual nobility is comparable to the semantic development of the English word gentleman.

One could ask whether Confucianism is not

Table for sacrificial offerings

merely a system of ethics and would therefore not warrant treatment in an outline of the religions of Korea. From several of Confucius' sayings we can draw the conclusion that he was only concerned with this world. Examples are "The Master did not speak of extraordinary things, feats of strength, disorder and spirits' (*Lun-yü* VII, 20); 'Tze-lu asked about serving spirits. The Master answered: 'When you are not yet able to serve men; how can you serve spirits?' Tze-lu asked about death and the Master told him: 'When you do not yet understand life; how can you understand death?' (*Lun-yü* XI, 11).

On the other side we find such sayings as 'He sacrificed to his ancestors as if they were present. He also sacrificed to the gods (spirits) as if they were present. He said 'When I am not present myself at the sacrifices, it is as if I had not sacrificed at all.' (*Lun-yü* III, 12). Confucius also speaks of T'ien (Heaven) as if it were an equivalent of Shang-ti (the supreme emperor, the supreme ruler of all destiny) and of T'ien-ming, the 'Mandate of Heaven': 'The gentleman stands in awe of the Mandate of Heaven' (*Lun-yü* XVI, 8).

Confucius' greatest follower, Meng-tze (Master Meng, Sino-Korean Maengja, 372–289 B.C.), latinized as Mencius, also frequently mentions T'ien and T'ien-ming: 'He who exerts his mind to the fullest will comprehend his own nature. He who comprehends his own nature, knows Heaven ... Everything is decreed by the Mandate [of Heaven]; one should obediently accept what has rightfully been concluded therein' (*Meng-tze* VII A, i, 1; ii, 1).

As early as 100 B.C. Confucius' adherents already had the custom of paying homage to him at specific times of the year. Since 72 B.C. ceremonies have been held not only for Master K'ung himself, but also for his 72 disciples. Hence a Confucius cult developed that one cannot help calling 'religious.' An Hyang (1243–1306) founded a Confucius Temple (Munmyo) in Korea in 1304. In its 'Hall of Great Perfection' the portraits of Confucius and his 72 disciples were worshipped.

In the eleventh and twelfth centuries a new philosophical direction developed in China. Though based on the teachings of Confucius and Mencius and with terminology borrowed from the Confucian classics, it owes its consolidation to Buddhism. This so-called Neo-Confucianism, an impressive system that comprises metaphysics, a doctrine of salvation,

personal and social ethics and political philosophy, culminated in the thought of Chu Hsi (1130–1200). His commentaries to some of the most important Confucian classics were officially recognized in 1313 as the correct interpretation of these works for the state examinations and remained the standard authority until they were abolished (in Korea in 1894, in China in 1905).

The introduction of the Chu Hsi School to Korea is attributed to the above mentioned An Hyang – probably incorrectly. Be that as it may, during the Chosŏn dynasty (1392–1910) Neo-Confucianism became the state doctrine, and school education all over the country was organized on the basis of this philosophy.

Unfortunately we will not be able to expatiate on the philosophical developments in Korean Confucianism during the Yi period. Let it suffice to mention the names of two important thinkers. Yi Hwang (pen name: T'oegye, 1501–1570) was the first Korean scholar to fully probe into the metaphysics of Neo-Confucianism and to be capable of developing them further. His great adversary was Yi I (pen name: Yulgok, 1536–1584). The polemics between the two led to the formation of two schools in which their respective disciples congregated. This split can be considered the original source of the fiercely contending factions that we described briefly in the chapter on history. This lamentable development notwithstanding, the Chosŏn period was the heyday of Confucianism in Korea and of the Chinese studies closely associated therewith.

Even after the demise of the Chosŏn dynasty the *sŏdang* or *kŭlpang* (Confucian private schools) continued to exist. In 1917 there were 25,485 *sŏdang* with 250,000 students, and in 1942 there were still 3,504 *sŏdang* with more than 150,000 students.

Although school instruction has been completely modernized in Korea, the ethics and morals of the people are still primarily shaped by Confucian views of the world and of life.

(upper row) *A memorial service honoring the Chosŏn kings and queens at Chongmyo. Chongmyo is the Chosŏn Dynasty's ancestral shrine, built to preserve royal ancestral spirit tablets. Dancers perform civil and military dances during the ceremony*

(lower row) *Sŏkchŏn, a memorial rite to venerate Confucius, is held at the Taesŏngjŏn of Sŏnggyun-gwan*

A Confucian scholar in Sangdŏk-sa

Sangdŏk-sa, 'Respecting Virtue Hall', of Tosan sŏwŏn,
the private school of the famous neo-Confucian scholar
Yi Hwang (1501-1570)

Family ancestor shrine in a private house in Yangdong,
Kyŏngsang Pukto

Bibliography

The following list of references contains only books written in the three so-called modern languages (German, English and French); journal articles are not mentioned.

General Works

CLAUDE BALAIZE, LI JIN-MIEUNG, LI OGG & MARC ORANGE, *La Corée (Que sais-je? 1820),* Paris 1991.

PAUL S. CRANE, *Korean Patterns,* Seoul 1967.

MARK DE FRAEYE, *Korea Inside, Outside,* Seoul 1990.

ECKART DEGE, *Kleiner Reiseführer Nordkorea,* Kiel 1991.

ECKART DEGE, *Korea, eine landeskundliche Einführung,* Kiel 1992.

ECKART & KATHERINE DEGE, cf. below, *sub* Lautensach.

RUDOLF GOOSMANN & ILSE MÜLLER-VON WERDER, *[Polyglott-Reiseführer] Südkorea,* München 1977.

A Handbook of Korea (Korean Overseas Information Service), Seoul 1990.

Korea (Insight Guides 6), Hong Kong 1981.

HERMANN LAUTENSACH, *Korea: Eine Landeskunde auf Grund eigener Reisen und der Literatur,* Leipzig 1945; translated as *Korea: A Geography Based on the Author's Travels and Literature* by ECKART & KATHERINE DEGE, Heidelberg 1988.

DOROTHY H. & WILLIAM D. MIDDLETON, *Some Korean Journeys,* Seoul 1975.

CORNELIUS OSGOOD, *The Koreans and Their Culture,* New York 1951.

RICHARD RUTT, *Korean Works and Days,* Seoul 1964.

W. SIEROSZEWSKI, *Korea, Land und Volk nach eigener Anschauung,* Berlin 1904.

S.E. SOLBERG, *The Land and People of Korea,* New York 1991.

YI KYU-TAE, *Modern Transformation of Korea,* Seoul 1970.

History

MARTINA DEUCHLER, *Confucian Gentlemen and Barbarian Envoys: The Opening of Korea, 1875–1885,* Seattle and London 1977.

HAN WOO-KEUN, *The History of Korea,* Seoul 1978[10].

JÜRGEN KLEINER, *Korea – auf steinigem Pfad,* Berlin 1992.

KI-BAIK LEE, *A New History of Korea,* Seoul 1984.

LI OGG, *La Corée des origines à nos jours,* Séoul/Paris 1989.

The North Korean standpoint is presented in:

INGEBORG GÖTHEL, *Geschichte Koreas. Vom 17. Jahrhundert bis zur Gegenwart,* Berlin 1978.

INGEBORG GÖTHEL, *Geschichte Südkoreas,* Berlin 1988.

Religion and Philosophy

ROBERT E. BUSWELL, *The Formation of Ch'an Ideology in China and Korea: The Vajrasamādhi-Sūtra, A Buddhist Apocryphon,* Princeton, NJ. 1989.

ROBERT E. BUSWELL, *The Korean Approach to Zen: The Collected Works of Chinul, Honolulu 1983.*

CHO HUNG-YOUN, *Koreanischer Schamanismus. Eine Einführung,* Hamburg 1982.

HUNG-YOUN CHO, *Mudang. Der Werdegang koreanischer Schamanen am Beispiel der Lebensgeschichte des Yi Chi-san,* Hamburg 1983.

CHOI MIN HONG, *A Modern History of Korean Philosophy,* Seoul 1980.

DIETER EIKEMEIER, *Elemente im politischen Denken des Yŏn'am Pak Chiwŏn (1737–1805),* Leiden 1970.

A. GUILLEMOZ, *Les algues, les anciens, les dieux,* Paris 1983.

HALLA PAI HUHM, *Kut: Korean Shamanist Rituals,* Elizabeth, NJ./Seoul 1982³.

Main Currents of Korean Thought, edited by the Korean National Commission for Unesco, Seoul/Arch Cape, Oregon 1983.

SPENCER J. PALMER, *Confucian Rituals in Korea,* Berkeley/Seoul, undated.

FRITS VOS, *Die Religionen Koreas (Die Religionen der Menschheit, vol. 22,1),* Stuttgart 1977.

BOUDEWIJN WALRAVEN, *Songs of the Shaman. The Ritual Chants of the Korean Mudang,* London and New York, 1994.

Art

ANDREAS ECKARDT, *Geschichte der koreanischen Kunst,* Leipzig 1929.

Kunstschätze aus Korea (Ausstellungskatalog), Hamburg/Köln 1984.

ALEXANDER B. GRISWOLD, CHEWON KIM & PIETER H. POTT, *[Kunst der Welt] Burma Korea Tibet,* Baden-Baden 1964².

W. B. HONEY, *Corean Pottery,* London 1955.

EVELYN MCCUNE, *The Arts of Korea. An Illustrated History,* Rutland, Vermont/Tokyo 1962.

H. ROUSSET, *Arts de la Corée,* Paris 1988.

PETER SWANN, *Art of China, Korea and Japan,* London 1967².

RENÉE VIOLET, *Einführung in die Kunst Koreas,* Leipzig 1987.

KEN VOS, *Korean Painting: A selection of eighteenth to early twentieth century paintings from the collection of Cho Won-Kyung,* London 1992.

Performing Arts

DIETER EIKEMEIER & MICHAEL GÖÖCK, *Getanzte Karikaturen. Traditionelle Maskenspiele in Korea,* Stuttgart 1988.

Language and Writing System

MAURICE COYAUD & JIN-MIEUNG LI, *Initiation au coréen écrit et parlé,* Paris 1982.

WOLFGANG FRANZ & REINER ITSCHERT, *Hun min jeong eum: Die richtige Laute zur Unterweisung des Volkes (1446),* Wiesbaden 1980.

KI-MOON LEE, *Geschichte der koreanischen Sprache,* Wiesbaden 1977.

BRUNO LEWIN & TSCHONG DAE KIM, *Einführung in die koreanische Sprache,* Heilbronn 1974.

LI OGG, KIM SUK-DEUK & HONG CHAI-SONG, *Initiation à la langue coréenne,* Séoul 1985.

WERNER SASSE, *Studien zur Entzifferung der Schrift altkoreanischer Dichtung 1; 2,1,* Wiesbaden 1988.

W. E. SKILLEND, *Early Readings in Korean,* London 1987.

Literature

PETER H. LEE, *Anthology of Korean Literature. From Early Times to the Nineteenth Century,* Honolulu 1981.

PETER H. LEE, *Poems from Korea. From the Earliest Era to the Present,* London 1974.

PETER H. LEE, *Korean Literature: Topics and Themes,* Tucson Arizona 1965.

MARC ORANGE & KIM SU-CHUNG, *Deux romans coréens du XVIIIᵉ siècle (Histoire de Dame Pak, Histoire de Suk-hyang),* Paris 1982.

MARC ORANGE, *Une femme à la recherche d'une illusion et cinq autres nouvelles,* Paris 1980.

INEZ KONG PAI, *The Ever White Mountain: Korean Lyrics in the Classical Sijo Form,* Tokyo 1965.

RICHARD RUTT, *The Bamboo Grove: An Introduction to Sijo,* Berkeley/Los Angeles/London 1971.

RICHARD RUTT & KIM CHONG-UN, *Virtuous Women. Three masterpieces of traditional Korean fiction,* Seoul 1974.

W. E. SKILLEND, *Kodae Sosŏl: A Survey of Korean Traditional Style Popular Novels,* London 1968.

HANS-JÜRGEN ZABOROWSKI, *Märchen aus Korea,* Düsseldorf-Köln 1975.

Colophon

Lay-out
    Antoon De Vylder, Zandhoven
Typesetting
    De Diamant Pers nv, Zandhoven
    Set in DTL Documenta, created by Frank Blokland.
Prepress
    Fotogravure Deckmyn en Co nv
    All photography using Agfa systems.
    Output using a SelectSet Avantra-imagesetter
    with MultiStar 600 RIP
    and CristalRaster screening technology
    onto Alliance film materials.
    Processed in Ecorap 72 on line processor.
    Proofing with Agfa XC707 colour copier/printer and Agfaproof.
Printing
    emico offset nv, Wommelgem
    Printed using Ozasol-offset plates
    on a Heidelberg Speedmaster 102F
Paper
    Donside Consort Royal Satin, 150 g/sm
Binding
    Splichal nv, Turnhout
    Brillianta linen
    Endpapers Yearling ECF smottled white, 120 g/sm